LEADERSHIP THEORY AND
THE COMMUNITY COLLEGE

LEADERSHIP THEORY AND THE COMMUNITY COLLEGE

Applying Theory to Practice

Carlos Nevarez, J. Luke Wood, and Rose Penrose

Foreword by Eduardo J. Padrón

STERLING, VIRGINIA

Published by Stylus Publishing, LLC
22883 Quicksilver Drive
Sterling, Virginia 20166-2102

Library of Congress Cataloging-in-Publication Data
Nevarez, Carlos, 1969-
    Leadership theory and the community college : applying
theory to practice / Carlos Nevarez, J. Luke Wood, and Rose
Penrose.—First edition.
        pages   cm
Includes bibliographical references and index.
ISBN 978-1-57922-631-2 (cloth : alk. paper)
ISBN 978-1-57922-632-9 (pbk. : alk. paper)
ISBN 978-1-57922-633-6 (library networkable e-edition)
ISBN 978-1-57922-634-3 (consumer e-edition)
    1. Community colleges—Administration.   2. Community
college presidents.   3. Educational leadership.   I. Title.
LB2341.N433   2013
378.1'11—dc23   2012030025

13-digit ISBN: 978-1-57922-631-2 (cloth)
13-digit ISBN: 978-1-57922-632-9 (paper)
13-digit ISBN: 978-1-57922-633-6 (library networkable
e-edition)
13-digit ISBN: 978-1-57922-634-3 (consumer e-edition)

Printed in the United States of America

All first editions printed on acid-free paper
that meets the American National Standards Institute
Z39-48 Standard.

Bulk Purchases

Quantity discounts are available for use in workshops
and for staff development.
Call 1-800-232-0223

First Edition, 2013

This book is dedicated to community college students who continue to confront a multiplicity of challenges. It is our hope that this text raises consciousness of the severity of issues that continue to inhibit their educational aspirations, persistence, and attainment while serving as a road map for college leaders to facilitate pathways for their success.

CONTENTS

ACKNOWLEDGMENTS

W e wish to thank the following case study contributors: Charles R. Mojock, president of Lake-Sumter Community College; JoLynn Britt, full-time faculty in liberal studies and credentialing at William Jessup University; Debbie Travis, president of Cosumnes River College; Deborah L. Floyd, editor in chief of *Community College Journal of Research and Practice* and professor of higher education leadership at Florida Atlantic University; Rivka Felsher, doctoral candidate at Florida Atlantic University; Jim Riggs, former president of Columbia College and professor of community college education at California State University, Stanislaus; Francisco Rodriguez, president/superintendent of Miracosta Community College; Edna V. Baehre, president of Central Pennsylvania's Community College; Regina L. Garza-Mitchell, associate vice president for student learning at Texas State Technical College; Pamela L. Eddy, associate professor of educational policy, planning, and leadership—higher education administration at The College of William and Mary; John D. Harrison, NCATE coordinator and assistant professor of education at Lincoln Memorial University; and Leila González Sullivan, former president of Essex Community College–Baltimore County and adjunct professor at North Carolina State University. We also wish to acknowledge Marissa Vasquez Urias, doctoral candidate, California State University, San Diego, for serving as a technical editor for several chapters.

FOREWORD

A recurring theme in my conversations with students over the years has been, "I didn't think I could do this." The doorways of the nation's community colleges have attracted countless students for whom a college education seemed out of reach. When they did arrive, their fragile confidence posed the first and often constant obstacle to success.

Many of those conversations, however, have had a happy ending as in, "Dr. Smith wouldn't let me walk away. I couldn't have done it without her."

Our students are Exhibit A that potential often wears the guise of inability or even failure. As leaders, we are surrounded by talent every day, some of it manifest, most of it veiled. And the simple truth that accompanies the men and women who have defined leadership is that no one does it alone.

Our colleges are renowned for crafting environments that counter the "I don't think I can do this" outlook. We challenge students, introducing new, demanding expectations. We also nurture and engage them, using the full playbook of approaches to mine their ability.

The great basketball coach John Wooden of UCLA won an unheard-of ten consecutive NCAA championships but never once used the word "win" to encourage his charges. And he chided them when they compared themselves to other players and other teams. He pushed them to prepare and practice, to stretch well beyond their own limited expectations. Wooden's practice sessions were transformative. Competitive greatness was first and only a matter of competing with yourself to become the best that you could be. And of course, this was not only transformative but also contagious. To couch it in another sporting idiom, the truly great players make everyone around them better.

Growth is, fundamentally, about leaving your comfort zone, time and again, and achieving just enough comfort with the uneven rhythm of change. The challenge of college leadership is not only to court classroom engagement, but moreover to invite the entire college community into the process. And more to the point, to promote ownership of the college's progress.

This is no small leadership assignment. It occurs at a moment when our institutions are in overdrive, central as never before to the future of the country and the lives of a new generation of college-going students. The challenge for every college leader today is to keep the engine humming while the many hands at the helm reconsider, together, the direction of the ship and then turn the required reflection into a dynamic community-driven movement.

Our institutions have always been fueled by a depth of sincerity and a feeling of reaching for something more. Our students model these traits, underdogs who are redefining higher education's impact on American society. Our advocacy on their behalf, our essential embrace of their needs, is the core of our community and the key to achieving broad ownership.

But there is urgency to this beyond the dictates of effective leadership. A college education is the required ticket to the mainstream economy and a meaningful, prosperous working life. The "right to fail" is an outdated maxim; student success demands that leadership in every aspect of the student experience be hands-on intrusive. And as we rethink and reinvent curriculum, teaching methods and student support, we're also auditioning leadership for a new era in higher education.

The word *entrepreneurial* does not have roots in American higher education practice, but it begs for clarity and a fair hearing today. Higher education, like every other planetary endeavor, is under pressure to integrate a relentless tide of technological advances that challenge hundreds of years of teaching and learning tradition. Retaining the integrity of that tradition as the classroom and basic relationships are redefined will require a new leadership skillset. Visionary, engaging, and team-oriented will be complemented by entrepreneurial and collaborative, a bridge builder to new partners. No one does this alone and no enterprise survives in isolation.

In the very near future, many of today's college leaders won't be doing this at all. Before the sendoff, however, it should be acknowledged that these men and women have presided over a remarkable transformation in the nation's colleges, including the expanded reach and diversity of higher education, elevated standards and an unprecedented level of respect for community colleges. But the average age of higher education's presidents today is 60 and climbing each year, according to the American Council on Education. More than half are 60 and older and only 8% are under the age of 50. But we are, indeed, surrounded by talent and our current efforts at reinvention are calling forth a new generation to navigate a new era. The chapters that follow will serve them well. I am betting they and a community of impassioned colleagues will be lifting lessons from these pages and applying them in ways we never dreamed.

Eduardo J. Padrón
November 2012

In 2005, the American Association of Community Colleges (AACC) released a report containing six core competencies for emerging and current community college leaders. They underscore vital areas of development needed for effective leadership in rapidly evolving institutions. These competencies are as follows:

1. *Organizational Strategy.* Leaders use the mission of the community college to drive institutional quality, protect and advance institutional practices, and hold constituents accountable for quality assurance while advancing the overall success of the institution.
2. *Resource Management.* The role of a leader is to support the operations of the community college mission by maintaining fiscal resources to support staff and system processes.
3. *Communication.* Community college leaders undertake honest and open dialogue, promote high expectations, and advocate for student success in the context of the community college mission.
4. *Collaboration.* Using a human relations approach (e.g., developing partnerships with internal and external constituents), leaders garnish support from multiple stakeholders to advance the community college mission.
5. *Advocacy.* Student success is promoted through the advancement of policies that encourage diversity, equity, inclusion, open access, and student learning.
6. *Professionalism.* Leaders undertake an ethical values-based approach (e.g., equity, honesty, caring) to advance a just institutional mission.

In this book, we integrate the AACC competencies and tie these guiding principles to leadership theory, case study analysis, and leadership inventories. For example, organizational dynamics are integral to several theories addressed in this text, including bureaucratic leadership, democratic leadership, political leadership, and transformational leadership. One of the competencies focuses on organizational strategy; in this case, several chapters depict various organizational constructs that leaders use to strategically guide their leadership. Table P.1 provides a matrix that leaders interested in connecting specific competencies to leadership approaches can readily reference.

These competencies are included in the text to reflect the established standards of the profession articulated by leaders in the field, serve as a framework to enable leaders to enact the community college mission, and provide a unified body of knowledge and skill sets relevant to sustaining and developing community college leaders. To be an effective leader, one must have specific knowledge; understand change and leadership theories; and cultivate essential skills, knowledge, and dispositions of the profession. McDade (1988) asserted that higher education will continue to face challenging times, thereby increasing the need for professional development opportunities to develop visionary leaders who can turn challenges into opportunities for quality institutional growth. In the same vein, Eddy (2010) noted that community colleges will face many new issues in the twenty-first century that will cause new tensions and challenge existing practices, processes, and structures.

TABLE P.1
Matrix of AACC Competencies and Leadership Approaches/Theories

Chapter	Organizational Strategy	Resource Management	Communication	Collaboration	Advocacy	Professionalism
3. Bureaucratic Leadership	☑	☑	☑		☑	
4. Democratic Leadership	☑		☑	☑	☑	☑
5. Path-Goal Leadership		☑	☑	☑	☑	☑
6. Situational Leadership	☑			☑		
7. Ethical Leadership			☑	☑	☑	☑
8. Leader-Member Exchange Theory			☑	☑		☑
9. Political Leadership	☑		☑	☑	☑	
10. Systems Leadership	☑	☑	☑	☑	☑	
11. Transformational Leadership	☑		☑	☑	☑	☑
12. Symbolic Leadership	☑		☑			☑
13. Transformative Leadership	☑		☑	☑	☑	☑

Therefore, understanding leadership frameworks (theory) in the context of case study analysis (practice), and self-introspection of one's own leadership style, becomes a critical component of leading community colleges. Given the current challenges facing community colleges, this intersection of theory and practice is essential for exceeding the standards of excellence embodied within AACC's core competencies.

While there is a multiplicity of theories surrounding leadership, this book focuses on the major theories that are most closely linked to AACC's (2005) six competencies. The theories presented herein reflect current leadership theories used to contextualize and resolve dilemmas facing community colleges. Many of these theories are guided by notions of equity, access, diversity, ethics, critical inquiry, transformational change, and social justice. The authors selected theories inclusive of these values that are most congruent in driving institutional change and, to a certain extent, challenging existing practices. Community colleges serve as the primary pathway, and often last opportunity, for an increasingly diverse student population, particularly students of color, low-income students, and first-generation college students (Bush, 2004; Bush & Bush, 2010). They also serve as an economic and workforce development engine for local communities. Leaders will actualize positive outcomes for their constituencies when they are educated in the theories, values, skills, and competencies embodied within this text. Unequivocally, the community college profession has come to a juncture where moving forward with a "business as usual" approach will not work. Internal and external forces are too great, demanding immediate transformation and change. This volume seeks to develop the "whole" leader through a threefold framework of theory, practice, and introspection in the context of institutional change. In doing so, leaders will be better equipped to lead community colleges in challenging times.

REFLECTIVE CASE LEADERSHIP FRAMEWORK

Community colleges, like many other postsecondary institutions, are in an environment marked by increased pressures for institutional (e.g., academic, structural, governance, infrastructure, financial sustainability) change. A number of external forces driven by public scrutiny, increased accountability, fiscal downturns, and evolving political landscapes are responsible for these pressures. To alleviate these pressures, leaders must strive toward actualizing student success (e.g., persistence, achievement, attainment, transfer), promoting workforce training, fostering economic development, serving the needs of the local community, and increasing transfer and terminal degree rates. This requires future leaders and administrators at each level of the community college hierarchy to use theory as a tool to guide their practice and, ultimately, transform their institutions. In doing so, leaders will be better able to understand the myriad viewpoints, factors, and intricacies associated with issues confronting community college leaders; organize various constructs (e.g., players, power dynamics, organizational culture, setting, unaccounted-for circumstances) associated with a given issue, providing them with a more comprehensive view of the complex challenges that they encounter; predict the potential outcomes of an issue, as well as actions of stakeholders; and control and guide stakeholders, processes, and structures to achieve desired outcomes. Utilizing theory in conjunction with case study analysis affords community college leaders with the tools needed to comprehensively interrogate and inform decision-making processes.

Case Study Approach

Through the analysis of case studies that deal with actual situations confronting today's community college (i.e., program development, demographics of the student body, staff recruitment and hiring, finance, political pressures, rural and urban community college students), the next generation of leaders will gain valuable insights that are typically learned only through experiential knowledge (i.e., on-the-job training). The cases presented in this book are based on real-life and fictionalized accounts of issues encountered by mid- and executive-level community college leaders throughout the nation. Great efforts were made to ensure that the cases presented are representative of the complexity of issues facing community college leaders (i.e., competing factors, ideologies, and demands). Thus, cases require readers to employ an advanced skill set (e.g., critical-analytical, human relations, political, emotional intelligence, problem resolution, conceptual, technical) while considering these competing interests to guide next steps in the decision-making process.

The benefits of using case study analysis in leadership development are numerous. They include exposing leaders to the predominant issues facing college leaders (e.g., accountability, fiscal constraints, diversity, governance), which may involve issues beyond their realm (e.g., region, position, institutional type); providing leaders with a platform to sharpen their problem-solving skills; allowing leaders to simulate the process of resolving a critical issue in a protected and supportive learning environment where errors can serve to further the learning experience without having detrimental effects on a career or an organization; and enabling leaders to engage in democratic (collaborative work) processes in which individuals are encouraged to present various perspectives with the ultimate purpose of arriving at sound resolutions.

Overall, using a case study approach challenges leaders to move beyond their understanding, preference, or level of comfort to consider alternative approaches to addressing problems that they face in their practice. Moreover, most leaders generally have not considered what type of leadership style they employ, let alone move beyond that style to use new paradigms. For instance, a leader may employ a bureaucratic framework, without understanding the implications, strengths, or weaknesses of that frame. A single frame carries with it a myopic approach to problem solving; however, the challenges that leaders face in their practice are complex and dynamic. Thus, to offset the limitations of using a single leadership approach, we call for a unified approach in which leaders employ multiple leadership lenses. These lenses, when used with intentionality, can result in more sound decisions.

However, successfully deploying multiple frames is easier said than done. This unified approach requires leaders to think beyond what they know; learn new ways of being; be open to new thoughts, dispositions, and models; and, most important, be flexible and adaptable to unforeseen and "never seen" challenges in the community college.

Nevarez-Wood Leadership Case Study Framework

Leaders should use the steps discussed in the following subsections in approaching a resolution to case study analysis, keeping in mind that the framework presented is multidimensional, fluid, cyclical, and nonstatic (see Figure 1.1). Moreover, it serves as a guide to facilitate effective and efficient case resolution. It is particularly important for community college leaders to

FIGURE 1.1
Nevarez–Wood Leadership Case Study Framework

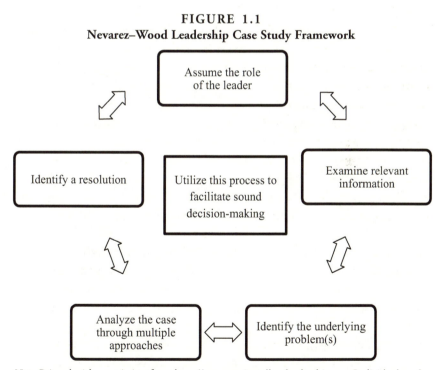

Note. Printed with permission from http://communitycollegeleadership.net. Individuals seeking supplementary resources (e.g., additional case studies, PowerPoint outlines of each chapter, leadership inventories, newsfeeds) should visit this website.

use the framework because it connotes the importance of reflective theory–practice whereby information considered, decisions made, and actions taken are continually and critically reflected on by leaders; it accounts for and provides guidance (a road map) in addressing the multiple missions of the community college, which include open access, comprehensive educational programming, serving the local community, lifelong learning, teaching and learning, and student success (see Nevarez & Wood, 2010); and the convergence of theory and practice integrated within this framework empowers leaders to make sound decisions.

What follows is a step-by-step process that enhances leaders' abilities to resolve complex and dynamic problems. Leaders may also reference Nevarez and Wood's (2012) "A Case Study Framework for Community College Leaders," which provides additional information about and contextualization of each step.

Step 1: Assume the Role of the Leader

There are two primary types of leadership approaches: informal and formal. Informal leaders gain their influence outside the formal authority, titles, or structure of an organization. Their power is vested by their peers who bestow upon them a sense of credibility, respect, influence, and backing. This, in turn, provides these leaders with considerable influence, including their commitment to the best interests of organization affiliates, people skills, knowledge, proven accomplishments, tenure, and insight to "getting the job done." By contrast, formal leaders are given organizational authority based on the power (e.g., rights, privileges, responsibilities) bestowed upon their position. The power and authority of holding a formal position is reinforced by the ability to serve rewards and punishments to subordinates. While leaders, through human relations, political maneuvering, and/or performance, may enhance their organizational power, the mere authority of their position demands a baseline of influence. When reading the case, we ask that leaders assume the formal role (e.g., president, vice president, dean, program director, department chair, faculty) of a leader who is able to influence the decision-making process. However, we ask that formal leaders consider how informal leaders can be allied with to support problem resolution and organizational success.

Although often used interchangeably, leadership and administration are two distinct concepts. Leadership is the act of "influencing and inspiring others beyond desired outcomes" (Nevarez & Wood, 2010, p. 57). Leaders are able to motivate their followers (through communication, interpersonal relations, vision, and investment in others) to meet the best interests of the organizations that they serve. In this approach, the relationship between the leader and the follower is one marked by collaboration; followers are often viewed as affiliates or teammates in the decision-making process. Administration refers to an autocratic approach for managing others. This approach relies on a hierarchical (top-down) style bolstered by the administrators' reliance on policy, rules, and procedures. In general, administrators manage their employees through a style that is controlling, directive, and restrictive in nature; thus, employees are viewed as subordinates. Some case studies will require leaders to assume the role of leader or administrator in decision making; whereas, others will require both approaches.

Step 2: Examine Relevant Information

Each respective case is informed by contextual factors. These factors are integral considerations in the decision-making process. Leaders should begin by identifying information presented in the case (e.g., setting, stakeholders, special circumstances). They should then delineate what information is key to case resolution. Leaders can use the following guidelines in examining relevant information:

1. List information contained in the case focusing on the setting, the stakeholders or groups involved, and special circumstances (e.g., unknown information, factors that cannot be planned for) surrounding the case.
2. Contextualize this information by providing substance to each point listed. Consider how the information identified is interconnected and influences the dynamics of the case. For example, when contextualizing information relevant to the setting, ask yourself: What is the climate of the institution? What is the demographic makeup of the individuals involved in the case? What are the normative behaviors, traditions, values, and institutionalized practices involved?
3. Reflect on what information is key to understanding and driving the resolution of the case. We suggest either circling or listing this information on a continuum ranging from least relevant to most relevant.

Step 3: Identify the Underlying Problem(s)

Community colleges are complex sociopolitical organizations. Therefore, the problems encountered by leaders in these organizations are often multifaceted and dynamic. In many circumstances, multiple problems are at play in a single case. Largely, there are two types of problems: primary problems (core issues) and ancillary problems (problems that are the by-products of primary problems). Often, leaders can get bogged down trying to treat ancillary problems without addressing the "root" issue at hand. For example, a community college may become concerned when its workforce development students are experiencing poorer than expected market outcomes (ancillary problems), such as low hiring rates of graduates, low job retention rates, low salaries, and low promotions; however, the root problem may be a disconnect between what is being taught in the classroom and what is expected in the market (e.g., too philosophical, outdated information, lack of relevancy, low applicability). When engaged in case resolution, leaders should consider the following steps:

1. Identify all the problems associated with a given case.
2. Identify the relationship (if any) between these problems.
3. Denote which problems are root problems and which are ancillary.
4. Use this information to drive the decision-making process, focusing on primary problems first and to a lesser degree on ancillary problems.

Step 4: Analyze the Case Through Multiple Approaches

This book presents multiple leadership approaches and theories. Readers are to use the leadership approaches provided in each respective chapter to address the cases presented. Each theory is undergirded by a philosophy of leadership values, which has direct implications for the "practice" of leadership. Further, each approach has associated strengths and weaknesses, depending on contextual factors relevant to each case. Astute leaders understand these strengths and weaknesses of each respective theory and are critical in the selection of the theory (or theories) that provides for optimal case resolution(s).

Having a cursory or surface-level understanding of each theory presented will provide only limited support in case resolution. Therefore, when reading each chapter, we suggest "getting into the theory"; by this we mean that readers must understand the intricacies, complexities, and nuances of the theory. This will require reading and rereading each chapter, ruminating on the elements of each approach. In doing so, readers must simulate the theory in its purest form, irrespective of their personal bias, disposition, perceptions, or initial inclination for case resolution. As leaders become more perceptive at case study analysis, they can also consider how multiple approaches may be fused or used simultaneously in the resolution of a case. The end goal is to ensure that leaders acquire the critical/analytical and problem-solving skills necessary for case study resolution. While constructs of multiple theories may apply, often one or two primary approaches best facilitate case resolution. For example, in a case study marked by loose policies, lack of adherence to rules or regulations, and fractured ties between and among subunits, a bureaucratic approach (focused on gaining control and direction through the use of directives, policy, rules, and authority) coupled with a systems approach (focused on the interconnectivity of departments) would enhance case resolution.

Step 5: Identify a Resolution

After taking into account the information from each respective step in the case study framework, leaders must identify a resolution. There are several options that can be employed to resolve a case:

1. Solve—an intuitive response, which can remedy the problem(s) without consultation
2. Resolve—the seemingly best course of action(s) based on evident contextual factors
3. Postpone—avoiding premature decisions, instead allowing time for reflection, data gathering, and planning
4. Redirect—delegating the resolution of an issue to another person, symbolically involving multiple stakeholders, or reconceptualizing the issue to present a new reality (i.e., spinning the issue)
5. No action—allowing time for an issue to either mature or resolve itself

Leaders should truly consider all potential outcomes. Often, inexperienced leaders are eager to solve or resolve issues without realizing the importance of postponing, redirecting, and avoiding action altogether.

2

ORGANIZATIONAL THEORY AND THE COMMUNITY COLLEGE

An Overview

Organizational theory attempts to describe the nature, behaviors, and structures of organizations and the individuals within them. This theory is used to inform and assess the operations, social dynamics, and future directions of organizations. Overall, organizational theory is concerned with the organization as a whole, including both internal and external influences ranging from the smallest details to the larger picture. In particular, scholars of organizational theory emphasize the interconnectedness of organizational dynamics (e.g., division of labor, governance, and policies), focusing on how these functions affect the organization itself and its stakeholders (Astley & Van de Ven, 1983; Hirsch & Lounsbury, 1997; Jones, 2007; King, Felin, & Whetten, 2010).

As a field of study, organizational theory is focused on several general areas: organizational development, organizational behavior, and organizational change. Taken together, these three areas examine the process by which organizations are built and sustained; how individuals act within organizations and are influenced by organizational processes, structures, and culture; and the manner in which organizations are modified and adapted over time. In general, there are several primary principles of organizations that allow researchers and practitioners to better understand the nature and importance of organizational theory. Understanding the value of the following principles empowers leaders to lead their organizations more effectively.

- *Interactive Systems.* We maintain that community colleges are interactive systems. In this light, the whole of each part (e.g., person, department) is dependent on other facets of the system. In an interactive system, relationships and processes are interwoven. Therefore, when one element of the system is not operating effectively, the entire system is affected. This system is linked through governance structures (e.g., policies, processes, and procedures), which serve to facilitate the realization of system goals (Marion, 1999a, 1999b; Marion & Uhl-Bien, 2001). For the community college, these goals represent the mission of the organization (e.g., open access, serving the local community, student success).

- *Formal and Informal Power.* Community colleges comprise both formal and informal power structures. Formal structures include the written policies, chain of command, and reporting processes. This information is usually transparent and readily available to organizational affiliates. By contrast, informal structures refer to power, insight, and information maintained and wielded outside of the formally designated structure. Informal power is obtained through reflective experience, understanding of organizational culture, perception of individuals' motivation, access to decision-making processes and/or decision makers, and socioemotional intelligence. For leaders to be successful in navigating the organization, they must be politically savvy, recognizing both forms of power (formal and informal) and understanding how each can be used to achieve organizational outcomes (Greve, 2007; Harrison, 1998; Mechanic, 1964).

- *Organizational Culture.* Each community college holds a distinctive organizational culture. Embedded within this culture are subcultures. These subcultures drive the overall trajectory of the college. Organizational culture is driven by values, dispositions, normative behavior, perspectives, accepted practices, protocols, habits of mind, and assumptions (Barney, 1986; Hatch, 2006; Jones, 2007). Organizational culture affects not only the productivity of the organization, but also the emotional health of those working for the organization. For community college leaders, it is important to connect affiliates through common commitments, goals, and the college mission (e.g., open access, comprehensive educational program, serving the local community). This in turn builds a sense of community, creating meaning for organizational affiliates while also increasing effectiveness.

- *Organizational Phases.* Organizations experience phases of development. Organizations are first conceptualized and then initiated. Once an organization is operating, negotiation of normative and acceptable behaviors occurs. Negotiated norms are implemented and efforts to reach maximum productivity follow a cyclical process. External pressures (e.g., budget crises, public demands) eventually impact the organization (McLeod, 2003); these factors affect the institution and force the institution to change. This is accomplished through a process of reinvention whereby a new way of being is conceptualized and then implemented. This process is cyclical, multidimensional, and dynamic. Reinvention in response to change leads to organizational vitality, viability, and productivity. Failure to do so jeopardizes the very existence of the organization itself, because changing environments require evolving organizations to meet additive demands, pressures, and conditions. As with other organizations, community colleges face external pressures that require them to reinvent themselves in order to meet the needs of the local communities that they serve.

• *Organizational Theory and Leadership Theories.* Organizational theory and leadership theories are interrelated concepts (Chance & Chance, 2002; Green, 2010). Organizational theory focuses on structures, policies, governance, power, interconnectivity, functions, and organizational processes. Organizational productivity is reliant on the maximization and alignment of these factors. As a living social organism, an organization relies on each unit (e.g., department, college), process, function, and individual to meet organizational goals (e.g., community college mission). Within each organization there is a delineation of power, with some individuals wielding greater levels of influence than others. Leadership theories are concerned with gradations of influence and how such influence is used to reap the most beneficial outcome for the organization. Thus, organizational theory and leadership theories provide "context" for understanding each respective body of theory. Just as organizational theory and leadership theories are mutually interconnected and interdependent, organizations and their leaders are as well. Effective leaders understand how institutions function and are able to direct their operations for the betterment of the organization. Because community colleges have multiple missions, leadership in these institutions is complex and dynamic. Therefore, the need to gain the skills, knowledge, and competencies of multiple leadership theories is a critical component of sound organizational decision making.

3

BUREAUCRATIC LEADERSHIP

Bureaucratic theory has its roots in the work of three scholars: Max Weber, Émile Durkheim, and Karl Marx. Each scholar wrote extensively about bureaucracy, organizations, and authority. The premise of bureaucratic theory is based on the grounds that organizational effectiveness is facilitated through strong processes, policies, rules, regulations, and protocols (Chance & Chance, 2002). Thus, bureaucratic leaders are *regulation oriented*. Their primary mode of apparatus centers on control over subordinates and the work environment through the standardization of guidelines, processes, and expectations. Consequently, the role of a subordinate is prescribed and often nonnegotiable. Hence, bureaucratic leaders are focused on individual and organizational *control*. Operating handbooks often accompany policies and procedures to further reinforce authority and power from above. These policies are designed to guide every facet of organizational behavior and functions. When a circumstance that lacks a clearly articulated policy is presented, new policies are implemented by managers to guide future actions, thereby avoiding organizational ambiguity. Typically, these policies are used to sustain and increase the control of authority within the organization (Hall, 1963; Mintzberg, 1979; Nevarez & Wood, 2010). Elements of bureaucratic theory must be employed for an organization to function because policies are needed to provide clarity to roles, responsibilities, and processes.

Bureaucratic tenets allow for institutions to have a scripted plan for reaching stated goals (typically referred to as a strategic plan) (Bensman & Rosenberg, 1960; Kotter, 1985). For example, many community colleges develop strategic plans with short-, mid-, and long-term objectives. When well crafted, these plans underscore the vision and mission of the institution. Further, the development and implementation of these plans are influenced by the bureaucratic nature of the institutional climate. This climate allows for the strategic plan to be advanced. Community colleges have numerous policies that guide all organizational functions, including retention, promotion, and tenure; student conduct; fiscal oversight; shared governance; admission requirements; academic standards; graduation requirements; due process procedures; course scheduling; federal and state reporting; and accreditation.

In an age of increased accountability, public scrutiny, and seemingly endless litigation, it has become even more critical for community colleges to adhere to the bureaucratic model. As a result of the unprecedented challenges that community colleges face (e.g., a greater emphasis on persistence and attainment rates, dwindling state funding, lack of understanding of the community college mission and functions, public reluctance to support postsecondary access), greater emphasis on a bureaucratic approach has been embraced. Further, given the numerous missions of the community college (e.g., comprehensive educational programming, lifelong learning, open access), a bureaucratic model is often used to allow institutions to efficiently meet the complex needs of their respective communities. To do so requires regulations that control the actions of personnel and the allocation of resources and services in accordance with the institution's strategic plan or stated goals.

Administrators who employ a bureaucratic model rarely solicit input from organizational affiliates or subordinates. In this approach, the primary responsibility of the leader is to oversee, document, govern, and determine the productivity of the worker. Paramount to this approach is the development, maintenance, and reinforcement of a stringent organizational structure. This is a by-product of a traditional *hierarchy*, which strives to perpetuate a top-down governance composition (Bass, 1985; Jackall, 1988). Therefore, making an allowance for shared decision making with subordinates would serve to weaken the administrator's authority. In essence, the bureaucratic model envisions social organizations as akin to an assembly line, in which human workers act and are expected to work like machines. To facilitate the activities and operations of the "assembly line," foremen (e.g., employers, supervisors) must maintain close watch over subordinates while continually reaffirming the importance of organizational hierarchy. As such, the bureaucratic model tends to reinforce current practices and is rarely supportive of innovation, especially from members of the assembly line whose input is not considered, sought out, or valued (Girodo, 1998; Weber, 1947).

In cases in which the organization is expanding or increasing in size (e.g., new programs, initiatives, or departments), line staff and managers (foremen) are added to the organizational structure. The addition of new line staff and managers is designed to advantage successive levels of the hierarchy, further enhancing management's control over the organization. Promotion of employees through the leadership ranks is based on their skills, abilities, competencies, support, and loyalty to the established hierarchy. These characteristics are assessed through standardized mechanisms of *productivity*. In pursuit of efficiency and greater control, managers often foster atmospheres that are hypercompetitive in nature, in which individual energies are focused on competing for greater levels of responsibility and authority (DiPadova, 1996; DiPadova & Brower, 1992).

Community colleges have strong hierarchies, often disguised as democratic in nature; in reality, these hierarchies are undergirded by bureaucracy. The president is the supreme authority within the institution, having the ability to make decisions on organizational direction, administration and staff employment, and most financial matters. Under the president is a host of senior executives (e.g., chief academic officers, vice presidents), midlevel leaders (e.g., assistant vice presidents, deans, department heads), and entry-level leaders (e.g., coordinators, directors) who "serve at the pleasure" of the president. Each of these staff members is subservient to a direct supervisor. Duties and responsibilities are associated with each position, allowing for organizational clarity and enhanced productivity. Job titles serve as an important symbol to project gradations of authority within bureaucratic structures, while serving as motivation for enhanced productivity and organizational commitment among subordinates.

In bureaucratic theory, organizational hierarchy is *vertical*. Communication is always directed upward, with orders to subordinates following a downward pattern. The quality of information being fed up the hierarchy is of particular importance to organizational efficiency and effectiveness. When incorrect or incomplete information is communicated upward to management, the directives from managers to employees are misguided, because there is a disconnect between managers and employees, whose roles are clearly defined and do not make allowance for relationships to be built across ranks. This restricts communication between employees and top managers. Rarely is information that is unrelated to direct orders fed downward unless it is designed to reinforce the hierarchy (Hatch, 2006). Further, informal horizontal transmission of information between midlevel managers is rare and unsupported. In such cases, the quality of communication between mid-level managers is reduced because clearly delineated roles inhibit the need for information sharing between ranks (Bass, 1990).

The tenets informing the conceptualization of bureaucracy are based on the following:

- employee skill levels and perceived abilities that inform the division of labor within organizations
- the establishment of a chain of command based on assumptions of inherent ability
- a set of protocols and regulations designed to control subordinates and to maintain social stratification
- an environment of austerity characterized by minimal communications, especially discourse between employees and employers
- a system of advancement, rewards, and punishments based on an allegiance to authority as well as support for and commitment to the organizational structure

There are numerous benefits for organizations utilizing a bureaucratic approach. First, clear protocols and regulations reduce organizational ambiguity. As such, information is readily available to organizational affiliates. Clearly delineated roles and protocols mean that workers can be more easily replaced. Second, accountability is increased as divisions of labor are known throughout the organization. Thus, when the "assembly line" does not operate at capacity, the problem in the line is easily detected and addressed. Third, human and financial resources are maximized, allowing for greater productivity. Finally, mechanized processes allow organizations to reduce human capital costs by hiring lower skilled and lower cost employees (Bensman & Rosenberg, 1960; DiPadova, 1996; Hatch, 2006).

Community college leaders can utilize the bureaucratic approach by establishing clear roles, responsibilities, expectations, and direction throughout the organization. This serves as a blueprint that guides all college affiliates in a unified direction. All affiliates clearly understand their role in contributing to the greater college mission. In laying out responsibilities through contractual agreements, organizational policies, and a traditional hierarchy, ambiguity is reduced. Strong policies and procedures better enable leaders to protect the organization from liability (Bass, 1990). This is a result of clearly delineated duties and responsibilities. For example, when guidelines for community college faculty clearly state expectations and requirements for promotion the institution is better protected from lawsuits initiated by faculty who failed to navigate these requirements. An additional example is the procedures that articulate the process by which confidential student information (e.g., social security numbers, grades, addresses) is transferred or protected between and among employees and departments. Academic honesty also is a contentious issue in higher education; many educators are concerned with issues of plagiarism, deception, and cheating. Strong academic honesty policies better allow institutions to uphold academic standards and increase efficiency in grade appeal and dismissal processes.

Discussion Questions

Consider the following questions in your analysis of the leadership theory presented in this chapter. In addition, pose your own analytical questions that will aid you in better articulating, analyzing, and critiquing the intricacies of this leadership theory.

- What are the strengths and limitations of bureaucratic leadership theory?
- What is the relationship between the leader and the follower in bureaucratic theory?
- How is influence gained, maintained, and extended in bureaucratic theory?
- How can bureaucratic leadership inform the resolution of critical issues faced by community college leaders?
- In what ways have you seen a bureaucratic approach employed within your organizational setting?
- How does your preferred leadership style compare to a bureaucratic leadership frame?
- In what ways (if any) could your personal leadership be enhanced by bureaucratic theory?
- In what way does bureaucratic leadership theory compare with and differ from other leadership theories presented in this book?

Dr. Charles R. Mojock
President
Lake-Sumter Community College

Partnerships: Campus Development in Tight Fiscal Times

Background

Lake-Sumter Community College (LSCC) is located in Central Florida, north of Orlando. The district was traditionally agricultural but recently has been changing rapidly into a suburban area with a large retirement population. The economic downturn hit the area hard due to its dependence on the housing boom. LSCC is a community college with a population of 4,750 students, an increase in enrollment of 34% over three years. While 71% of the students served are Caucasian, African American students make up about 11% of the enrollment and Hispanic student numbers have doubled over the past five years to about 12%. The college is a unique community college district comprising of three separate demographic regions spread over two counties. There is no single, large-scale industry or a significant center of population. On the north end of Lake County, the population is predominantly retired citizens. On the west is Sumter County, rural and predominantly agricultural. On the south end of Lake County, the college's campus serves an urbanizing population, much younger, that is largely dedicated to commuting to Orlando for jobs, recreation, and services.

For the past three years, three of the major district institutions—the college, South Lake Hospital (a private nonprofit arm of Orlando Health Corporation), and the Lake County District School Board—have been engaged in developing plans for a medical magnet high school academy to be housed on the South Lake campus of LSCC. The purpose of the academy is threefold: (a) it will resolve the shortage of qualified health care employees now plaguing the medical establishment in the county, (b) it will establish a higher level of high school education and reduce dropouts, and (c) it will improve the delivery of health care to the county's senior citizens.

Currently, the South Lake Campus is the college's "partnership" campus, housing three successful partnership facilities: a joint public-college library in cooperation with the Lake County Commission, a joint-use education building in cooperation with the University of Central Florida, and a joint-use softball field complex with South Lake Hospital's National Training Center. To date, two principle planning documents have been completed and executed by all three institutions: a Memorandum of Understanding and the more detailed Interlocal Agreement. The plans call for a $3 million contribution from the Lake County School Board and a $1 million contribution from South Lake Hospital to be used for instructional laboratory equipment. The college's contribution to the project was the provision of 10 acres of campus land. The detailed agreement specified that the monetary contributions be used to draw down state matching funds, enabling LSCC to construct a much needed health-science building while the school board would construct the facility for the high school health academy. A joint architectural selection process was completed, and the exchange of the deed to the land for the $3 million between the college and the school board has been completed.

Statement of the Problem

The severity of the nation's economic downturn has been amplified in Florida, causing drastic budget cuts at all levels of public enterprise. The Lake County School Board has been forced by its necessary budget cuts to halt the further development of this joint project. The state of Florida, facing severe revenue shortages, also has mandated budget reductions and restrictions, which have included the elimination of capital outlay expenditures for public building construction and the further suspension of the Florida's Matching Fund Program as well. The health academy is now on hold.

You are the president of LSCC and must now decide on a future course of action to recommend to the college's board of trustees. There are several difficult options that remain:

- Do nothing and await the return of fiscal support from the legislature, recognizing that once the project begins there will be a minimum of three additional years to design, build, and occupy any new facility once funding is available.
- Agree with the Lake County School Board that the project be permanently suspended and pursue capital outlay funds for your health-science building independently from other sources.
- Pursue other public partnerships that might produce the required matching funds in keeping with the board of trustees' vision of partnership development on the South Lake Campus.
- Pursue private entrepreneurial and investment opportunities. The prime location of the South Lake Campus (10 acres of lake shore property) can be promoted to lure sound investment.

Nevarez & Wood–Bureaucratic Leadership Inventory (NW-BLI)

This leadership inventory is designed to assess the degree to which a leader adheres to a bureaucratic frame. Current leaders should reflect on actions that they typically take and perceptions that they hold. For aspiring leaders, conceptualize how your actions in formal (e.g., work) and informal (e.g., home, extracurricular activities) settings may determine your degree of bureaucratic influence. Be sure to consider what your actions are, not what you would like them to be. Read the following statements and mark the appropriate response following your instinct; there are no right or wrong answers. Key: 1 = Strongly Disagree, 2 = Disagree, 3 = Somewhat Disagree, 4 = Somewhat Agree, 5 = Agree, and 6 = Strongly Agree.

	Strongly Disagree	Disagree	Somewhat Disagree	Somewhat Agree	Agree	Strongly Agree
1. Organizational success is facilitated through strong policies and protocols						
2. Organizational success is facilitated through a strong chain of command						
3. Leaders should have complete control over their employees						
4. Organizational success necessitates that processes and structures are efficient						
5. It is the leader's responsibility to enact new policies when there are areas where policies are not evident						
6. It is the leader's responsibility to direct and the follower's responsibility to carry out their orders						
7. Leaders should have complete control over the organizational environment						

8. Organizational success is achieved through the pursuit of productivity							
9. Handbooks, frameworks, and organizational documents should clearly delineate each individual's areas of responsibility							
10. Employees should never circumvent the organizational structure							
11. Rewards are used as a tool to control employees							
12. Employee advancement should be based solely upon measures of productivity							
13. Policies drive organizational practices							
14. Collaboration inhibits organizational success							
15. Punishments are used as a tool to control employees							
16. Employee worth is primarily measured through productivity							

Note. This inventory is printed with permission from the Nevarez-Wood Community College Leadership Institute. All rights reserved.

Scoring

To score your responses, add your responses to all of the statements in the inventory. This is your total bureaucratic leadership score. Higher scores indicate greater levels of bureaucratic orientation, whereas lower scores indicate lower levels of bureaucratic orientation. The maximum score possible is 96.

_____ Total Bureaucratic Administrative Score

Score Meaning

While the maximum score is 96, many leaders may desire to understand their usage of this framework in comparison with that of other leaders. To facilitate this interest, scores from prior inventory participants were divided into percentile ranges. These percentile ranges allow leaders to understand their score in relation to the scores of other leaders. The percentile ranges are as follows: Low bureaucratic orientation (25th percentile or lower), Medium bureaucratic orientation (26th to 50th percentile), High bureaucratic orientation (51st to 75th percentile), and Very High bureaucratic orientation (76th to 99th percentile).

- Low bureaucratic orientation: 16–46 points
- Medium bureaucratic orientation: 47–53 points
- High bureaucratic orientation: 54–62 points
- Very High bureaucratic orientation: 63–96 points

Improve Your Bureaucratic Administrative Score

Regulation Orientation. Develop and facilitate procedures, protocols, rules, and regulations for effective use of human efficiency and maximization of resources and services.

Hierarchy. Provide subordinates with specific work performance goals and objectives while monitoring their work. In doing so, determine how you can support their goal achievement (e.g., allocation of resources, motivation, support).

Control. Develop and support a system of supervising progress, providing precise feedback, and holding subordinates accountable for performance.

Productivity. Learn skills and techniques for delegating work according to the skills and expertise of subordinates. In delegating work, assess goal attainment progress.

Reliability

Two internal consistency estimates were employed to examine the reliability of the bureaucratic leadership inventory: split-half coefficient and coefficient alpha. For the split-half reliability, the scale was divided into equal halves for item equivalency. We took into account the order of the measures; thus, the sequence of items was rotated. One half consisted of items 1, 3, 5, 7, 9, 11, 13, and 15 and the other half consisted of items 2, 4, 6, 8, 10, 12, 14, and 16. The

split-half coefficient was .86 and the coefficient alpha was .88. Both procedures illustrated satisfactory reliability. To view this inventory or learn more
about using the inventory for research purposes, see http://community
collegeleadership.net.

Suggested Reading

Nevarez, C., & Wood, J. L. (2011). *Nevarez & Wood–Bureaucratic Administrative
Inventory (NW-BAI)*. Sacramento, CA: Nevarez-Wood Community College
Leadership Institute.

4

DEMOCRATIC LEADERSHIP

The democratic model is based on McGregor's (1960) Theory Y suppositions, in which leaders use their influence to encourage participation, support employees' efforts, and encourage employees to assert their input toward accomplishing organizational goals. Under the democratic approach, the motivation, interests, involvement, and aspirations of employees are viewed as paramount to employees functioning as a team. Group decision making underscores democratic leadership. A venue for input and solicitation of thoughts and problem-solving skills is welcomed and encouraged. In doing so, time and space is created within the organization to reflect, dialogue, and solicit various perspectives (Apple, 2000; Pateman, 1983). This ultimately results in the deliberation of a multiplicity of perspectives that leads to a unified decision. The decision is considered unified when the majority of participants agree to support the decision, and the minority agree to disagree and commit themselves not to impede actions taken in carrying out the decision (Beane & Apple, 1999).

The governance structure of community colleges clearly delineates democratic tenets. This is primarily illustrated through faculty senate processes in which each academic unit within the institution has representation. For example, in soliciting changes to curricular matters, there are a multiplicity of committee levels (department, college, university-wide) charged with reflecting and deciding on the matter. These committees work as a team to consider every facet of the curricular request and ultimately make a group decision on the matter.

Moreover, the values embedded within a democratic model engage participants in the decision-making process. The tendency is for leaders to view employees as an asset and, in doing so, use their life experiences, skill sets, and expertise as tools in guiding organizational practices and change. When a true democratic environment is established, organizational affiliates gain a sense of responsibility, ownership, and buy-in, subsequently working beyond their contractual obligations to "give back" to the organization (Nye, 2008; Starratt, 2003). Employees are trusted to do "right" for themselves and the organization. This is practiced through the honor system. This independence further propels employees to work toward greater efficiency and effectiveness. In essence because employees feel valued and trusted, they are motivated to give more (e.g., energy, time, resources) to the organization (Fishkin, 1991). In turn, the leader/organization makes a commitment to develop employees via professional development opportunities. In cases in which employees are slacking off and not fulfilling their roles and responsibilities, the greater majority ultimately decides their fate (e.g., demotion, ostracism, dismissal). The ramification of not working to fulfill one's responsibility tied to the greater group is typically harsh.

Leaders using the democratic model focus on the interests of organizational affiliates by supporting professional development of staff, continually providing them with feedback for improvement, and using a collaborative form of leadership as a means to share power. This approach is widely accepted in community colleges, particularly among faculty, to promote shared governance. In an effort to support the concept of shared governance, leaders secure the consent and voice of those whom they govern through participative processes. This is done through formal (e.g., faculty senate, town hall meetings) and informal (e.g., small-group discussion, one-on-one conversations) processes (Bell, 1950; Woods, 2004).

Democratic leadership maintains traditional hierarchies found in most organizations. This approach does not seek to overturn these traditional structures, powers, or mores; on the contrary, it seeks to make them more democratic. In an autocratic system, decisions are made and implemented from a top-down bureaucratic approach. By contrast, democratic leadership merges working relationships between leaders and organizational affiliates (Dahl, 1989; Hellriegel & Slocum, 2009). Finding a balance between hierarchy and democratic structures maintains institutional functions; informs institutional affiliates of their responsibilities and roles; and embraces institutional change, creativity, and collectivism. This balance also facilitates buy-in among stakeholders in decision making and enables a system of checks and balances to be employed. This unified approach can allow institutions to function effectively and efficiently and to actualize their respective institutional goals. Although using democratic leadership as the primary leadership approach can be time-consuming, the benefits of having collective input are great (e.g., more harmonious work environments, employee empowerment, shared responsibility for negative outcomes, more robust responses to institutional challenges).

There are three general benefits to the democratic approach. First, respect, trust, and equitable treatment of followers are reciprocal and permeate the social fabric of the organization (Starratt, 2003). Through the accepted governance structure in community colleges (e.g., faculty senate, student government, academic committees, community task forces), policies, systems, and processes are negotiated and agreed upon. Second, as the organization grows and becomes more complex, followers' decision-making abilities are valued (Fishkin, 1991; Lewin, 1950; Pateman, 1970). Given the multiple missions of the community college (e.g., open access, student success, comprehensive educational programming, serving the local community, lifelong learning, teaching and learning), numerous functions must be simultaneously carried out. With limited availability of resources and personnel, confidence in leaders' abilities, as a result of shared decision making, serves to build the leadership capacity of the institution. Therefore, as turnover occurs, expansion takes place, and multiple pressures are placed on community colleges (e.g., budget constraints, accountability pressures, legislative mandates). Thus the development of capable and multiskilled leaders can ensure a smooth and efficient transition of power. Third, when leaders incorporate staff as members of a team, employee morale increases as their input, expertise, and experience is valued by leadership. Overall, this can create a positive work environment where college affiliates feel a sense of empowerment, ownership, and satisfaction. In turn, these affiliates are more likely to go beyond the call of duty to reach organizational goals.

There are three significant bases of democratic leadership specific to community colleges. First, there is a wide belief that if leaders treat organizational affiliates in a cooperative approach, they will, in turn, treat others (e.g., students, community members) accordingly. Second, the increasing complexity, fluidity, growth, and multiple missions of community colleges make these organizations difficult to manage by a handful of leaders. Thus, dependence on organizational affiliates to take on leadership positions, such as department chairs, program coordinators, and college deans, is encouraged and welcomed by democratic leaders. The notion of shared leadership becomes central to the governance structure of community colleges in that team leadership becomes paramount in running an institution. Third, the college environment, under a democratic approach, increases the quality of relationships among individuals within the organization and leads toward a more inclusive environment. In this environment, organizational affiliates feel a sense of community and are valued, respected, and encouraged to do well for themselves, the institution, and the overall community (Court, 2003; Haiman, 1951; Kutner, 1950).

Discussion Questions

Consider the following questions in your analysis of the leadership theory presented in this chapter. In addition, pose your own analytical questions that will aid you in better articulating, analyzing, and critiquing the intricacies of this leadership theory.

- What are the strengths and limitations of democratic leadership theory?
- What is the relationship between the leader and the follower in democratic theory?
- How is influence gained, maintained, and extended in democratic theory?
- How can democratic leadership inform the resolution of critical issues faced by community college leaders?
- In what ways have you seen a democratic approach employed within your organizational setting?
- How does your preferred leadership style compare to a democratic leadership frame?
- In what ways (if any) could your personal leadership be enhanced by democratic theory?
- In what way does democratic leadership theory compare with and differ from other leadership theories presented in this book?

JoLynn Britt
Liberal Studies and Credentialing
William Jessup University

Issues of the Athletic Department

Background

Gold River Community College is a state-funded, two-year community college located near a large metropolitan area in Northern California. The college serves more than 35,000 part-time and full-time students. The student population is 49% White, 13.8% Hispanic, 8.4% Asian, 8.4% African American, 2% Filipino, 1.2% Native American, and 17.2% other. More than 40% of the population is in the age range of 18–24. The college offers associate's degrees in both the arts and sciences as well as various vocational certificates in a total of 70 career fields. It also offers transfer education in which students complete freshman and sophomore course work, and then transfer to a four-year college or university.

Gold River Community College offers numerous sports for its students, including football, volleyball, cross country, men's and women's soccer, baseball, softball, swimming, and tennis. The college has a high participation rate among students in campus athletics compared with other community colleges its size, partly due to its recruitment program. In addition, the college ranks ninth in the state for its overall win/loss record among all other community colleges in its division.

Statement of the Problem

You have just been hired as the new vice president of the college, and your first task is to address the numerous and complex problems within the athletic department. There are various issues within the department that have gone unresolved for a number of years, and tensions among the athletic director, coaches, and physical education staff are escalating. The president of the college has made it clear that he expects you to bring a timely resolution to these issues, indicating that if things do not start turning around rather quickly, you may be out of a job. Additionally, you learn that the burnt-out athletic director is not interested in working with you or even talking to you and that he appears to have a hopeless and disgruntled outlook on the approaching athletic season. Prior to your arrival, the president requested a progress report on the current status of the department from the athletic director. You have been asked to review this report and then schedule a meeting with the athletic director to begin addressing the needs and conflicts within the department. The report addresses problems related to budget allocations, academic policies for athletes, and policies related to Title IX under federal law. The following information is presented in the report:

- *Budget.* In an effort to minimize tensions among the coaching staff, the athletic director has allocated equal amounts of money to each sport. Although the coaches of the swim team and cross country team feel that they have adequate financial support, Coach Meyers, the popular head football coach, has complained numerous times that his sport requires more money than the others because of the high overhead of equipment such as helmets, jerseys, pads, training equipment, and travel costs. The football team also has the highest number of team members, compared with the other sports on campus. Coach Meyers feels that his players have missed many important opportunities because he has had to limit the team's participation in numerous invitationals and events outside of the area due to lack of travel funds. He argues that the football budget should naturally be larger than the cross country budget because the football team has a greater number of players and the equipment and travel expenses are greater than that of the cross country team. He is threatening to quit if changes in the budget are not made by the start of the next football season. Replacing the head football coach would be devastating to the team and the community.

In addition to the objections raised by the head football coach, other coaches are complaining about the equity of salaries and workload within the athletic department. Some of the coaches argue that they are working much longer hours than the physical education instructors and, consequently, should be paid more. Some of the coaches' schedules involve time spent recruiting, teaching classes, conducting daily practice, and traveling and competing with their teams on weekends. On the other hand, some of the noncoaching physical education staff are instructors who teach a few classes a week and have no evening or weekend obligations to their jobs. Such disparity is causing friction within the department.

- *Academic Policies for Athletes.* The college has a strict policy requiring all athletes to maintain a minimum GPA of 2.5 in order to compete. Whereas the probation status of students in sports that utilize individual competition, such as swimming or cross country, does not directly affect the team as a whole, this is not the case in team sports such as soccer or football, in which the absence of a key player directly affects the overall performance and morale of the team. Coaches for the team sports have expressed the need for additional academic support/tutoring programs for their students who are falling behind. Although the college provides some academic support/tutoring programs, they are offered only in the afternoon hours when all the athletes are at practice. The dean for academic affairs has already expressed that it would be unfair to change the hours of the current academic support programs just to meet the needs of student athletes. This declaration is compounded by the fact that there are no additional funds or available staff to extend these services. Thus, the coaches for the team sports wish to use the general athletic department budget to pay for additional academic support services. By contrast, the coaches for individual sports do not see the need for such services and believe that it is the responsibility of the students, not the athletic department, to maintain proper academic status and seek out help on their own time, if needed. This disparity among the coaching staff is contributing to the increasingly tense atmosphere within the department.

• *Equity and Title IX.* There have been growing tensions within the athletic department related to the policy surrounding Title IX of the Education Amendments of 1972. Title IX, a U.S. law enacted on June 23, 1972, states: "No person in the United States shall, on the basis of sex, be excluded from participation in, be denied the benefits of, or be subjected to discrimination under any education program or activity receiving Federal financial assistance" (U.S.C. § 20). The softball coach is threatening to file a formal complaint against the department alleging unfair practice regarding gender equity governed by Title IX. Coach Morgan, the softball coach, has complained numerous times that the baseball team has newer equipment than the softball team and fields that are larger and better maintained than the softball fields. In addition, Coach Morgan believes the department spends more time on recruitment and media outreach for the baseball team than it does for the softball team. Coach Morgan attributes the high success of the baseball team to these issues and argues that the softball team is being unfairly discriminated against. The athletic director dispels any unfair treatment by the department, claiming that the baseball coach has spent a great deal of time organizing fund-raisers to purchase new equipment and has made a personal effort to reach out to the media and regularly invites them to games and functions. Furthermore, the athletic director reports that it is simply logistics that the baseball team has the newer fields because those fields accommodate both a larger team and a larger crowd.

After carefully reviewing this report and thoughtfully considering each issue presented, reflect on how you could move forward with your task of working with the athletic department to address the aforementioned problems. Consider the following:

- What are both the professional and financial needs of each coach on staff and how can they be supported by the department?
- What financial support for the department could you propose with the current budget limitations?
- How can the department provide support for both students and their coaches when the athletes are in danger of academic probation?
- What are the responsibilities of the department in terms of clarifying and providing equity and equal opportunity to coaches and students as protected by Title IX?
- What steps should be taken if a formal complaint is filed by a coach against the department under the law of Title IX?

Nevarez & Wood–Democratic Leadership Inventory (NW-DLI)

This leadership inventory is designed to provide a personal profile of democratic leadership. It consists of statements that denote behaviors, thoughts, and dispositions contained within the tenets of democratic leadership. Current leaders should reflect on actions that they typically take and perceptions that they hold. Aspiring leaders should consider the actions that they would take if they held a formal leadership position within an organization. Read the following statements and mark the appropriate response; if you find statements difficult to answer, trust your instinct and judgment in selecting the most appropriate for you. Remember that there are no right or wrong answers. Key: 1 = Strongly Disagree, 2 = Disagree, 3 = Somewhat Disagree, 4 = Somewhat Agree, 5 = Agree, and 6 = Strongly Agree.

	Strongly Disagree	Disagree	Somewhat Disagree	Somewhat Agree	Agree	Strongly Agree
1. I prefer/enjoy collaborating with others					*5*	*(6)*
2. I prefer/enjoy investing in the personal and professional development of my staff					*5*	
3. I believe that collaboration (e.g., working in teams, committee-work) is vital to organizational success					*5*	
4. I believe that collaboration leads to the 'best' decisions				*4*		
5. I regularly provide and support learning and development opportunities for my staff						*6*
6. I am known for engaging others in shared decision making						*6*
7. I prefer/enjoy community-building at work					*5*	
8. I value the experience, insight, and knowledge of my staff					*(5)*	*6*
9. I spend a lot of time building a community/family-like atmosphere at work					*5*	

the best?

10. I believe that building a sense of community at work is vital to organizational success					5	(6)

Scoring 5 | - 53

To score your responses, add your responses to all of the statements in the inventory. This is your total democratic leadership score. Higher scores indicate greater levels of democratic orientation, whereas lower scores indicate lower levels of democratic orientation. The maximum score possible is 60.

_____51-53___ Total Democratic Leadership Score

Score Meaning

While the maximum score is 60, many leaders may desire to understand their usage of this framework in comparison with that of other leaders. To facilitate this interest, scores from prior inventory participants were divided into percentile ranges. These percentile ranges allow leaders to understand their score in relation to the scores of other leaders. The percentile ranges are as follows: Low democratic orientation (25th percentile or lower), Medium democratic orientation (26th to 50th percentile), High democratic orientation (51st to 75th percentile), and Very High democratic orientation (76th to 99th percentile).

- Low democratic orientation: 10–47 points
- Medium democratic orientation: 48–52 points
- High democratic orientation: 53–57 points
- Very High democratic orientation: 58–60 points

Improve Your Democratic Leadership Score

Collaboration. Increase your association with organizational affiliates by actively engaging yourself at all levels of the organization, while learning to listen actively and considering different points of view.

Capacity Building. Consider undertaking professional development opportunities, such as leadership trainings, courses, institutes, and fellowship programs. Increase job responsibilities that lead to skill development and enhancement.

Community Building. Involve others in setting goals for the institution, developing a plan for meeting them, determining whether goals are being met, and making decisions based on group input. Create an affirming environment where employees are treated with respect and care.

Reliability

Two internal consistency estimates were employed to examine the reliability of the democratic leadership inventory: split-half coefficient and coefficient alpha. For the split-half reliability, the scale was divided into equal halves for item equivalency. We took into account the order of the measures; thus, the sequence of items was rotated. One half consisted of items 1, 3, 5, 7, and 9 and the other half consisted of items 2, 4, 6, 8, and 10. The split-half coefficient was .89 and the coefficient alpha was .88. Both procedures illustrated satisfactory reliability. To view this inventory or learn more about using the inventory for research purposes, see http://communitycollegeleadership.net.

Suggested Reading

Nevarez, C., & Wood, J. L. (2011). *Nevarez & Wood–Democratic Leadership Inventory (NW-DLI)*. Sacramento, CA: Nevarez-Wood Community College Leadership Institute.

5

PATH-GOAL LEADERSHIP

P ath-goal theory centers on an assortment of leadership behaviors used to motivate employees to accomplish desired goals. Leaders align their leadership approach to motivate employees in accordance with the needs of work situations. Leaders utilizing this theory are well versed in a variety of leadership approaches and behaviors (House, 1996; Schriesheim & Schriesheim, 1980). It is paramount that path-goal leaders be insightful; self-confident; sociable; highly intuitive; and able to evaluate and interpret the skills, proficiencies, and dispositions of employees (Jermier, 1996; Wofford & Liska, 1993). These skills enable leaders to employ a leadership style that will most likely motivate employees toward desired actions to facilitate organizational goals.

Within the constructs of the path-goal theory, leaders utilize one of four leadership styles (directive, supportive, participative, achievement oriented) to motivate and create pathways for goal attainment. The leader behavior utilized is dependent on four primary factors: the situation, the needs, the environment, and the characteristics of employees. The situation refers to the intricacies and nuances of the issue at hand, dilemmas, challenges, or goals that have created a need for enhanced employee productivity. Needs refers to the barriers (e.g., mental competencies, skills, resources, policies, structures) that are inhibiting or limiting employee efficiency. The environment refers to contextual factors in the college, including the climate, culture, mores, power relations, and dispositions of employees and their respective subunits. Characteristics refer to socioemotional intelligence, competence, perceived ability, tenure, weaknesses, and other attributes of the employee. Using this information, effective leaders employ leadership styles that serve to create pathways for employees to achieve desired outcomes/goals (Evans, 1970, 1996; House, 1971, 1996; Kroll & Pringle, 1985).

When employing path-goal theory, leaders select among four leadership approaches to utilize with each employee: directive, supportive, participative, or achievement oriented (Fulk & Wendler, 1982; Jermier, 1996). The leader utilizes a *directive* style by defining the procedures, rules, and desired outcomes for situations requiring explicit directions. Such directions are typically accompanied by strict deadlines denoting when tasks need to be completed, as well as continual supervision on the part of the leader. This style of leadership is often needed when the goals are ambiguous, the employee is inexperienced, the task is highly complex, or the employee is unmotivated. The leader utilizes a *supportive* style by maintaining an open-door policy that is friendly and empathetic. Values of respect, equitable treatment, and the creation of a sense of belonging for all employees underscore this leadership style. This approach is effective when subordinates are certain of their capabilities but may feel unsatisfied by the repetitiveness of their work routine. In this case, the leader provides nurturance to ensure that employees feel a sense of affiliation. The desired outcome of the supportive leadership approach is to promote greater psychosocial satisfaction among employees. Path-goal leaders may also integrate the *participative* leadership style in which they encourage employees to engage in the decision-making process. This is accomplished through the solicitation of perspectives, opinions, and ideas that are authentically integrated into decisions that guide institutional processes. This approach is best used when employees are skilled, seasoned, and experts in their respective posts. The *achievement-oriented* leadership style is used when employees are encouraged and supported to meet and exceed high standards. This is achieved partially by the leader expressing his or her confidence in employees to reach their maximum potential and seek continual improvement. The leader utilizes a variety of psychological strategies to ensure that employees have a high degree of confidence in their abilities, knowledge, and conceptual and technical skills in accomplishing goals. This style also is used when employees are seasoned and/or highly competent and/or need to be challenged to reach greater horizons (House, 1996; House & Mitchell, 1974; Schriesheim & DeNisi, 1981; Schriesheim & Von Glinow, 1977).

Path-goal theory provides leaders with a system that is flexible and enables them to assess the needs of their staff and support them effectively. For example, new faculty who lack experience would require a more directive leadership approach, in which the leader provides clearly communicated responsibilities, instructions on how to meet professional goals, and institutional requirements. By contrast, tenured faculty would require an achievement-oriented approach that is aligned with challenging faculty to reach beyond their typical mode of operation (Evans, 1996; House, 1996; Jermier, 1996). The end result is that employees feel a renewed sense of interest and purpose in their profession. This leads to enhanced relevancy, currency, and dedication to the field, enabling faculty to advance their practice (e.g., teaching, service, scholarship), thereby better fulfilling the needs and interests of the leader and the institution. Community college leaders must communicate high expectations that infuse the college mission (e.g., open access, teaching and learning, student success, comprehensive educational programming) and provide for the allocation of resources, which can set the path for employee success.

Path-goal leadership theory is dynamic. It may be appropriate to use more than one approach with a single individual; as such, this approach can pose increasing complexity for the leader. When selecting the leadership approach, the leader will provide the employee with support in determining goals, eliminating obstacles, and obtaining resources as necessary (Wofford & Liska, 1993).

Path-goal theory seeks to create positive alignment between the employee and the leadership style undertaken by the leader. This, in turn, promotes high employee motivation, productivity, and satisfaction. A negative alignment between leadership style and the employee can produce amotivation, inefficiency, low morale, and dissatisfaction. Thus, it is of critical importance for leaders to correctly assess contextual factors relevant to a given environment, employee, and circumstance. Using this contextual information, the leader either engages in or abstains from intervening. This decision is based on the employee's level of productivity, motivation, character, and contribution to the overall success of the team. When intervening, the leadership approach selected must be aligned with the contextual factors as assessed by the leader. Employee motivation in response to the leadership style applied can fall somewhere within the continuum of the positive and negative outcomes (Evans, 1996; Fulk & Wendler, 1982; Schriesheim & Neider, 1996). The leader needs to be aware that motivation is not constant; continual assessment of employee motivation and satisfaction is necessary in order to ensure proper alignment between leadership style and the employee (see Figure 5.1). Leaders therefore need to continually measure outcomes and

FIGURE 5.1
Conceptual Depiction of Path-Goal Theory

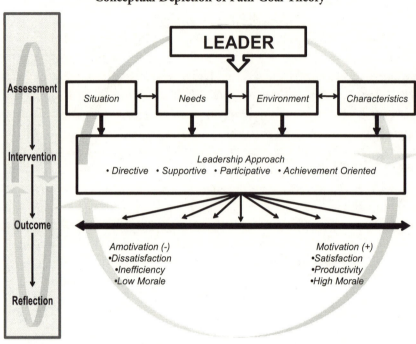

reflect on the effectiveness of employee performance and level of motivation. This reflection is necessary in part because of the evolving nature of contextual factors (e.g., employee knowledge, skills, disposition, and tenure). In turn, this reflection will provide space for the leader to discern whether he or she has accurately gauged the needs, characteristics, environment, and situation relevant to the employee. Further, leaders can then ascertain whether the leadership approach employed was the most appropriate given the context and whether new approaches should be used in the future (House, 1971; House & Mitchell, 1974; Jermier, 1996).

Discussion Questions

Consider the following questions in your analysis of the leadership theory presented in this chapter. In addition, pose your own analytical questions that will aid you in better articulating, analyzing, and critiquing the intricacies of this leadership theory.

- What are the strengths and limitations of path-goal leadership theory?
- What is the relationship between the leader and the follower in path-goal theory?
- How is influence gained, maintained, and extended in path-goal theory?
- How can path-goal leadership inform the resolution of critical issues faced by community college leaders?
- In what ways have you seen a path-goal approach employed within your organizational setting?
- How does your preferred leadership style compare to a path-goal leadership frame?
- In what ways (if any) could your personal leadership be enhanced by path-goal theory?
- In what way does path-goal leadership theory compare with and differ from other leadership theories presented in this book?

Deborah L. Floyd
Professor, Higher Education Leadership and
Editor in Chief
Community College Journal of Research and Practice
Florida Atlantic University

Rivka Felsher
Doctoral Candidate
Florida Atlantic University

Caught in the Middle

Background

Creative Community College (CCC) is a medium-sized, suburban, comprehensive community college with a for-credit enrollment of 7,500 students, the majority of whom attend part-time. The college also enrolls nearly 4,000 noncredit students annually, with classes offered on two additional satellite campuses in rural communities in the CCC service area. The CCC student demographic reflects the demographic of local communities, with 35% African American, 20% Latino, and 3% Asian American students enrolled. A growing number of younger students are enrolling as a result of state universities raising their tuitions and admissions requirements. Most residents do not view the college as one of first choice but more as a junior college for students who cannot attend a state university for reasons of geography, academic preparation, and cost. Most of the noncredit course enrollment is in areas of job training and workforce development, although the college also offers a series of popular special-topic courses on a variety of subjects of interest to many retirees and sponsors after school programs for area youth.

CCC is a public, primarily state-supported college with a seven-member, locally elected board of trustees. The president reports directly to the board of trustees, although the state governance system has recently been changed "again" so that a new State Board of Education may have certain control or influence over issues of faculty union employment and contract negotiations. For now, however, faculty contracts are negotiated at the local college level. The local board of trustees is a governing board with responsibilities for hiring and firing the president with select oversight from the state board.

CCC was founded 30 years ago and had two presidents prior to the arrival about a year ago of Dr. Mary Margaret Dynamo, a middle-aged Caucasian female with a doctorate in higher education leadership and a background in English teaching. President Dynamo was the first choice of the faculty during the search process, largely because she demonstrated a strong vision for moving the college curriculum forward in innovative ways. She also had a professional history of working her way up from a faculty member to administration, so the faculty felt she could relate well to them. Another characteristic that the faculty found attractive was her feisty leadership style.

During the interview processes she emphasized that she believes strongly that leaders should follow Kouzes and Posner's (2003) exemplary leadership practices especially in areas of challenging processes, inspiring a shared vision, modeling the way for others, and enabling others to be successful. Faculty appreciated that she backed up her leadership vision with a research-based theoretical model that could be taught and implemented collegewide. Although some now grumble privately about hiring a woman for the job, most faculty like her leadership style. President Dynamo respects the faculty and meets with them often, and she also accepts invitations to speak to classes, developing her relationship with students and increasing her visibility. She frequently reiterates that she believes strongly in shared governance and academic freedom. Overall, the president appears to be committed to ethical leadership practices, and to the public it appears that she practices what she preaches.

President Dynamo spends a lot of time with her board members, encouraging them to learn more about and implement Carver and Carver's (1994) model of policy governance for community college boards. She meets with some resistance, but a handful of board members are receptive to making incremental change in this area. However, the recent change in board membership, including the election of four new members and a new board chair, has resulted in a setback in her efforts to improve board relations and effective governance. Nevertheless, she is resilient and persists in her efforts.

President Dynamo has appeared at local community fund-raising events as well as created workforce education partnerships with local school boards and industries to improve town relationships, particularly in the area of traffic control around the main campus, and environmental cleanup and community beautification projects. Local news media coverage of the president is mixed, but generally favorable. The media have yet to delve into her personal life.

Statement of the Problem

Until recently, the board of trustees has not been directly involved in major academic policy and practice decisions, although the board clearly complied with the legal aspects of approving budgets, curriculum and program plans, and other issues as required by law. The new chair of the board, John Johnson, is a wealthy, elderly, Caucasian financial entrepreneur who strongly believes that the college should be run "like a business." Chair Johnson is one of the four new board members, and rumor has it that the college administration and local community have surmised that he "bought his way" into being elected into the position of board chair. More than half of the trustees strongly support Chair Johnson's move toward accountability and business methods of running the college, although they have not clearly articulated all aspects of their vision and plans for implementation. The board has been clear that the graduation rate at CCC is way below expectations; only 37% of entering freshmen graduate with an associate's degree, and of those who do graduate only 41% transfer to a four-year college or university. These statistics are not new and this has been an ongoing concern of the college for years. According to Chair Johnson, "It is entirely unacceptable that the student product outputs are so dismal. Something must be done. Faculty must be held accountable." Outside formal meetings, Chair Johnson has been quite vocal about his belief that faculty have a "cushy" job because they teach only about 20 hours per week and then go home to play golf and otherwise enjoy leisure activities.

During a regularly scheduled board meeting, President Dynamo was given her "orders" by the board. In response to the college's institutional effectiveness report that included student matriculation and graduation data, Chair Johnson exclaimed, "Develop an incentive plan to fix this problem! Faculty must be held accountable or we will need to get a new president of this college!" He further exclaimed that his employees report to work 40-plus hours per week and, thus, college faculty should do the same. While some board members seemed rather shaken and intimidated by the new board chair's declarations, none contradicted his directive to President Dynamo that she bring a plan to the board at the next meeting outlining the problem and solutions for how she will make the CCC faculty more accountable.

Also sitting on the board is local media company owner/publisher Jamie Ortiz-Smith, whose empire, Smithsonic, includes a tricounty newspaper (also online and with a print and an electronic Spanish edition); five local town papers (each with a Facebook page); a local TV news channel (also on Twitter); and classic rock, country, and Latino music radio stations. Jamie is watching this story closely. Not surprisingly, the tricounty newspaper reports this story on the front page and prominently in its online edition just hours after the meeting. The following day, television and radio stations lead their morning-drive-time news with the story that the new board of trustees of CCC is united in making college faculty accountable for dismal student retention and graduation rates. Before noon, an Associated Press reporter, Guy Breezy, who also works for Smithsonic, calls the college and asks to speak to President Dynamo about this new order for accountability, but she is attending a Rotary luncheon and unable to respond. However, the college media representative tells the reporter, "President Dynamo appreciates the trustees' guidance and plans to address their requests in due time."

The "micromanagement" by the new majority of the board of trustees of a suddenly "urgent" issue—an issue that has in fact existed for a long time—is surprising to the administration, although many are saying that this is just a "wait-and-see" thing in terms of how President Dynamo will deal with the challenge. They are counting on her defending the faculty's rights and academic freedom.

Mohammad al-Musa is the president of CCC's faculty senate, a unionized group. Dr. al-Musa had called an emergency meeting of the senate following the board meeting; the members of the senate are outraged regarding the unsupported blame being placed on faculty. Next to the elevator of the administration building, President Dynamo saw an announcement that local and national union representatives, Janet Powers and Nigel Thrace, respectively, would be in attendance. Rumor has it that Janet and Nigel are poised for intervention. Prior to the faculty senate meeting, the union leadership contacted the president to learn her position. The union leaders believe that holding faculty accountable for student graduation rates violates their contract and they expect President Dynamo to get the board off their back immediately. The faculty leadership is particularly concerned about the local media and their ability to turn the community, and thus the board of trustees, against the rights of the faculty, who are currently in negotiations with administration regarding contract revisions.

Tyler Jackson, vice president for academic affairs and one of the attendees at the senate meeting, is afraid of becoming the scapegoat in this situation. Tyler's ambition is the college presidency; he was a finalist for President Dynamo's position. He does not believe his career can afford to take a hit at this juncture. President Dynamo is not confident in his loyalty or ability to serve in his position and is expecting him to provide data and options to help solve the problem.

President Dynamo calls an emergency meeting of all the vice presidents, deans, and department chairs for the following day at 8:00 a.m. She believes that she is caught between supporting and defending faculty and appeasing a rather hostile board of trustees, especially the new chair. She describes the problems and the directives of the board of trustees to the administrative leadership and asks for guidance.

Questions

- Who are the principal players and major stakeholders in this case? What are the competing interests? What forces are at play?
- How can this case be viewed through the lens of the community college change model? How does the setting impact the case? What are the special circumstances of this case that influence the players' actions so far, and their potential decisions going forward?
- What are the underlying problems overall in this case? What are the challenges? What might have caused the sudden turn of events by the board of trustees?
- Do you believe that the president is "caught in the middle"? Why or why not? Who else might be caught in the middle?
- What should President Dynamo say or do in the meeting with her senior leadership?
- What should she do about the negative press she is suddenly receiving?
- What advice for handling the situation do you have for each of the other principal players? How can the community college achievement gap model be employed in this case, and by whom?
- What theories and leadership principles are at work from the different perspectives of the principal players?

- What legal precedence might apply in this case? What rights to "due process" do the faculty have?
- How can the problem be solved, resolved, postponed, redirected? Is no action appropriate? Why or why not?
- How might each player make his or her decision? What decisions and outcomes would be most beneficial to each of the principal players?
- How can a sense of team build on the leadership capacity of the faculty and administration to improve overall institutional effectiveness?

Nevarez & Wood–Path-Goal Leadership Inventory (NW-PGLI)

This leadership inventory is designed to aid leaders in assessing the components of path-goal leadership. Path-goal leaders are known for assessing organizational landscapes and people and using specific leadership approaches to motivate employees to meet desired goals. Current leaders should reflect on actions that they typically take and perceptions that they hold. Aspiring leaders should consider the actions that they would take if they held a formal leadership position within an organization. Read the following statements and mark the appropriate response. Key: 1 = Strongly Disagree, 2 = Disagree, 3 = Somewhat Disagree; 4 = Somewhat Agree, 5 = Agree, and 6 = Strongly Agree.

	Strongly Disagree	Disagree	Somewhat Disagree	Somewhat Agree	Agree	Strongly Agree
1. I regularly engage staff in group decision making						6
2. I make it a point to be encouraging to my employees					5	
3. I set challenging goals for employee performance				4		
4. I foster an affirming environment among my staff					5	
5. I motivate staff to accomplish desired goals					5	
6. I am explicit about my expectations for employee conduct					5	
7. I keep my staff "in the loop" at all times					5	
8. I make sure that my staff has all the resources they need to excel at work						6
9. I consult staff for their perspectives and insight					5	
10. I constantly push my staff to go beyond set expectations				4		

Scoring

To score your responses, add your responses to all of the statements in the inventory. This is your total path-goal leadership score. Higher scores indicate greater levels of path-goal orientation, whereas lower scores indicate lower levels of path-goal orientation. The maximum score possible is 60.

_____*50*_____ Total Path-Goal Leadership Score

Score Meaning

While the maximum score is 60, many leaders may desire to understand their usage of this framework in comparison with that of other leaders. To facilitate this interest, scores from prior inventory participants were divided into percentile ranges. These percentile ranges allow leaders to understand their score in relation to the scores of other leaders. The percentile ranges are as follows: Low path-goal orientation (33rd percentile or lower), Medium path-goal orientation (34th to 66th percentile), and High path-goal orientation (67th to 99th percentile).

- Low path-goal orientation: 10–46 points
- Medium path-goal orientation: 47–52 points
- High path-goal orientation: 53–60 points

Improve Your Path-Goal Leadership Score

Motivation. Read books and attend leadership trainings to improve the way you motivate and lead others. Leaders align their leadership behavior approach to motivate employees in accordance with the needs of employees and work situations.

Multiskilled Orientation. Learn about many leadership approaches. Leaders utilize a variety of leadership styles to motivate and create pathways for goal attainment. Participate in leadership development trainings, institutes, and seminars to gain greater familiarity with leadership approaches.

Assessment of the Situation. Establish a systematic approach of assessing the overall needs of individuals. Leaders must assess issues faced along with the needs and characteristics of the employees involved and then select the appropriate leadership approach to guide employee behaviors and actions.

Support. Facilitate employee success by encouraging employees to reach their potential, while providing pathways toward greater professional growth. Allocate resources and services that can set the path for employee success.

Reliability

Two internal consistency estimates were employed to examine the reliability of the path-goal leadership inventory: split-half coefficient and coefficient alpha. For the split-half reliability, the scale was divided into equal halves for item equivalency. We took into account the order of the measures; thus, the sequence of items was rotated. One half consisted of items 1, 3, 5, 7, and 9 and the other half consisted of items 2, 4, 6, 8, and 10. The split-half coefficient was .94 and the coefficient alpha was .90. Both procedures illustrated satisfactory reliability. To view this inventory or learn more about using the inventory for research purposes, see http://communitycollegeleadership.net.

Suggested Reading

Nevarez, C., & Wood, J. L. (2011). *Nevarez & Wood–Path-Goal Leadership Inventory (NW-PGLI)*. Sacramento, CA: Nevarez-Wood Community College Leadership Institute.

6

SITUATIONAL LEADERSHIP

Situational theory is a leadership principle that connotes that the best course of action is based on the situation and its given circumstances. In this theory, leaders first determine what the best outcome is for the organization. This necessitates what is referred to as consequentialist or "ends-based" thinking. From this perspective, the most effective decision for the organization does not focus on set rules, procedures, or codes in place. Instead, the best decision is based on what is perceived by the organization's leader(s) as the best outcome for the organization in its effort to resolve situations (Blanchard, Zigarmi, & Nelson, 1993; Yun, Cox, & Sims, 2006).

Scholars of situational theory suggest that four important contextual factors must be taken into consideration when assessing a situation. First, *the relationship between leaders and members* in the organization must be considered. Understanding the complexities of social interactions within the organization will better allow leaders to determine which leadership approach is needed at a given time (Graeff, 1983, 1997; Northouse, 2007). For example, lack of efficiency within a given department may require a more bureaucratic approach in which policies, guidelines, and expectations are clearly delineated. When working with seasoned employees with ample organizational knowledge, a democratic style may be more beneficial, allowing the leader to draw from staff expertise.

Second, leaders should have a clear understanding of the *task at hand*. Leaders must be able to define the task (e.g., problem, issue, concern) effectively. Tasks can range from high to low structure. High-structure tasks are rudimentary in nature, meaning that the process for completing the task is very linear and systematic. This allows for a clear assessment of whether the task was successfully accomplished (Norris & Vecchio, 1992; Vecchio, 1987). An example of a high-structure task is a college admissions process in which students must first apply to the institution, complete assessment tests, participate in an orientation, meet with counselors, and then register for classes. Although the order of steps can vary by institution, the adherence to these steps is prescribed (Vecchio, Bullis, & Brazil, 2006). Often, there are processes with checks and balances in place to ensure that a student has completed a step prior to moving on to the next step. Male student initiatives, which are organized efforts to improve the enrollment, persistence, graduation, and transfer of male students, are examples of low-structure tasks. The manner in which these efforts can be undertaken varies greatly. In essence, there is no step-by-step process or correct way of engaging in an initiative. Some colleges host events, others sponsor clubs, and some initiatives are more research-based; whereas, others rely on experiential knowledge (Nevarez & Wood, 2010).

Third, the *degree of authority* held by a leader as dictated by the position is important to consider. This power is acquired by formal and informal mechanisms. Formal power is derived from the inherent duties, responsibilities, and purview of a given leadership position. This authority is bestowed upon leaders by the greater governance structure and institutional hierarchy (Graen, Alvares, Orris, & Martella, 1970; Houghton & Yoho, 2005). Examples of this formal power are the ability to hire and fire, allocate awards, and enact punishments. Informal power is gained through human relations skills, which draw on networks and influence others to guide organizational decision-making processes. Relationships are built with employees by advocating for their interests, providing them with emotional support, allocating resources necessary for them to complete tasks, and including them in decision-making processes.

Finally, the leadership style employed should consider the *level of maturity* of each respective employee. Assessing an employee's level of maturity is based on two primary factors: their willingness to engage in the task, and their ability to complete the task. Both of these factors range on a separate continuum, which must be understood by the leader (Blank, Weitzel, & Green, 1990; Cairns, Hollenback, Preziosi, & Snow, 1998). For example, in an optimal situation, an employee will have a high level of both ability and willingness to accomplish organizational objectives. However, in reality, some employees will have a high level of ability but a low level of willingness, and other employees may have a low level of ability but a high level of willingness. Further, employee ability levels and workplace dedication are often dynamic; thus, depending on a given time period, circumstance, or task, each employee's level of workplace maturity and dedication can be in flux. Correctly gauging this level of maturity allows the leader to select the most appropriate leadership approach to facilitate self-dependent and self-motivated employees who can accomplish goals (Fernandez & Vecchio, 1997; Goodson, McGee, & Cashman, 1989).

Situational theory assumes that although there are many possible ways of addressing a situation, there is one theory or approach that is more aligned than the others. Using this approach, leaders should consider the intended outcome and compare alternative courses of action in order to select the best approach based on the circumstances impacting the situation (Graeff, 1983; Houghton & Yoho, 2005; Vecchio et al., 2006). Situational theory relies on an appropriate assessment of circumstances in a given situation. A monostyle approach to leadership is not sufficient in addressing the dynamic, multidimensional, and complex nature of social organizations and the actors within them. This theory requires leaders to have an astute awareness of multiple leadership styles, approaches, and theories. This knowledge will enable leaders to consider the strengths and weaknesses of implementing different approaches based on contextual factors. Such awareness facilitates leaders' consideration of alternative courses of action during decision making, thereby facilitating their selection of the most appropriate approach.

Discussion Questions

Consider the following questions in your analysis of the leadership theory presented in this chapter. In addition, pose your own analytical questions that will aid you in better articulating, analyzing, and critiquing the intricacies of this leadership theory.

- What are the strengths and limitations of situational leadership theory?
- What is the relationship between the leader and the follower in situational theory?
- How is influence gained, maintained, and extended in situational theory?
- How can situational leadership inform the resolution of critical issues faced by community college leaders?

- In what ways have you seen a situational approach employed within your organizational setting?
- How does your preferred leadership style compare to a situational leadership frame?
- In what ways (if any) could your personal leadership be enhanced by situational theory?
- In what way does situational leadership theory compare with and differ from other leadership theories presented in this book?

Jim Riggs
Former President, Columbia College
Professor of Community College Education
California State University, Stanislaus

Part I: When Troubles Just Keep Getting Worse: The Missteps of Two Senior Administrators in Handling Problems With a Basketball Coach

Background

Chamberlin Valley College (CVC) is a comprehensive community college with its main campus located in a farming and ranching community in a northwestern state. The college serves approximately 5,000 students each semester, with 75% of the student body of traditional college age, ranging from 18 to 25. More than 85% of the students graduated from area high schools. The community of 25,000 has had a strong tradition of supporting school sports at all levels, including the athletic programs at the community college. The men's basketball team at CVC, with a historically strong winning record, including one state championship, has been a particular source of pride for the community.

In recent years, however, the basketball team has had problems, leading to two consecutive losing seasons. This losing streak has caused a fair amount of public criticism of the coach and the former college president, including some scathing editorials. The community is tight-knit, and residents did not have any qualms about contacting members of the board of trustees to voice their displeasure over the team's losing record. Key athletic supporters and donors in the community continued to put pressure on the coach (also a tenured faculty member) to develop a stronger team and bring back "the winning tradition."

When the president suddenly left the college earlier in the year, the board appointed the vice president for student services (VPSS) as the interim president. The vice president has been at the college for nearly 10 years and is generally well respected by the faculty, staff, and the community. Since accepting the interim position, she has openly expressed her ambition to become the permanent president. In the past, she has had a number of conflicts with the men's basketball coaches and dislikes the current coach, who has been in his position for five years. Two years prior, the former president moved all the athletic programs to the instructional division as a result of the ongoing conflict between the VPSS and the coaches. The vice president of instruction (VPI) is in his third year in the position and has general responsibility for the athletic program. However, the direct supervision of the athletic program is the responsibility of the dean of arts and sciences, who is in his first year as an educational administrator.

One day, as the VPI returns to his office after attending a lunch meeting in town, his secretary informs him that she just received a call from the mother of one of the basketball players. She reports that the mother was extremely angry with the basketball coach because "the coach quit paying the electric bill for her son's apartment." The VPI replies that it is against the statewide Committee for Athletics to provide assistance to athletes that is not available to all other students. The VPI assumes that there must be a problem between the mother and her son, and that the son most likely spent the utility money on something else and made up the story about the coach. Later, the mother shows up on campus and tells the VPI about the coach's broken promises to support her son while he is attending college and playing basketball. She accuses the coach of cutting off support for her son because he is angry that the team lost several games this season and is trying to teach the players a lesson. When questioned about the truthfulness of her story, the mother says that the coach is the one who made initial contact about playing basketball at the college. She also states that the coach promised to cover the tuition, fees, book expenses, and living expenses including rent and utilities, and that her son would receive a weekly food allowance. She adds that the money is supposed to come directly from the coach and assistant coaches.

The VPI immediately contacts the dean who supervises the athletics program to find out what he knows about the situation. The dean is unaware of any specific promises made to any players but indicates that the college's business officer has reported a number of basketball players being behind on their tuition payments. In addition, the work-study payroll time sheets for the basketball players appear to have an excessive number of hours, considering that they are in the middle of basketball season.

The dean and VPI meet with the basketball coach early the following week. Prior to the meeting, the dean sent the coach an e-mail listing the concerns. At the meeting, the coach denies any recruitment violations, indicating that all the basketball players contact him first. The coach insists that the only thing he has done is encourage the students to file for financial aid to help cover their tuition expenses and other costs. He says that he told the players there is a work-study program so students can earn money while going to school. Then he assures the VPI and dean that he made no promises to any of the players or their parents regarding him personally paying for school-related or living expenses.

Following the meeting, and in response to the ongoing problem of the basketball players not paying their tuition bills, the business officer institutes a policy requiring that all athletes pick up their financial aid grant checks in person at the business office, and that if they owe money to the college, it will be deducted from their checks. The coach tells the business officer that he is aware that some players are behind on their tuition payments, and that it is the fault of the business office for not mailing the financial aid grant checks to the students. In response to the work-study hours claimed by some of the basketball players over the past two months, the coach becomes agitated and states that the work-study funds are allocated to the students and they can work when it suits them.

The VPI directs the dean and coach to prepare a brief response to the mother's concerns because the VPI will need to brief the interim president on this matter. Within two days the dean and coach provide what appears to be a logical point-by-point rebuttal to the mother's concerns. The VPI sighs with relief that he can put the matter behind him and decides not to bring the problem to the attention of the interim president because, based on her reactions to past issues, he knows she does not like to hear about problems, especially with any of the men's sports programs. The interim president also is well known for a micromanagement style that antagonizes many of the administrators, and the VPI does not want her trying to manage what appears to be a nonissue with the coach.

Statement of the Problem

The VPI receives a call from the regional athletic conference commissioner outlining his meeting with the mother who has alleged that her son is being denied financial support to play on the basketball team. He states that if what she is alleging is true, the team will be required to forfeit all its games for the past two years and could receive other major sanctions (including a very large fine) for violating the athletic commission rules. The VPI quickly agrees to start an investigation. Without notifying the interim president, he hires a retired university athletic director to conduct an investigation of the basketball program. Because of her background as a head coach of a university women's basketball team, he thinks she will be well received by the basketball coach. The VPI is certain there are no major problems to be found.

Within a week, the investigator contacts the VPI and dean to schedule a meeting to review her findings. At the meeting, the investigator discusses several areas of concern. She reports that after interviewing all the current basketball players, many of their parents, and several former basketball players, she found a clear pattern of recruitment violations, inducements, and unfulfilled promises of financial support from the coach and his assistants. The investigator provides the VPI with a written summary of the findings. She says that in her assessment these violations have been going on for years and are part of the routine operating procedures not only for the coaches at CVC but for the coaches at other colleges in the athletic conference. She feels that there are deeper and more serious problems with the basketball program. Although she does not document this in her report, she informs the VPI and dean that in addition to the recruitment violations, there has been systematic misallocation of federal work-study funds and college money allocated to the basketball program, and that payroll and financial documents appear to be routinely falsified.

She tells the VPI and dean that multiple basketball players told her that the coach and his assistant set up a system in which they have students sign blank work-study payroll time sheets and travel reimbursements. The coach fills in the hours and amounts on the time sheets and travel reimbursements and then has the checks sent to the home address of the assistant coach. The checks are brought into the coach's office, and each player is called in one at a time and directed to endorse the payroll and travel reimbursement check over to the coach. The coach then takes the endorsed checks to the bank and cashes them. The money is supposed to be used to pay the living expenses of the players, but the investigator notes that a number of the players complained that they never saw the money, or that the coach routinely threatened to quit paying their rent and utility bills if the team did not start winning.

After the meeting with the investigator, the VPI calls the coach into his office to respond to the investigator's report. The coach becomes very defensive and complains that the investigator is biased against men's sports. The coach further tries to justify his actions by stating he is managing several players' money at their request. The VPI asks the coach to provide an accounting of all the funds he has been handling for the students.

The VPI takes the investigator's report to the interim president, who is angry with him for not bringing this problem to her attention sooner. She is concerned that this could become a public relations nightmare. Five of the seven trustees are up for reelection in the fall, and any adverse publicity could seriously jeopardize their chances of being reelected. She also is planning to go to the voters in the spring to get approval for a capital construction bond. She tells the VPI, "If I am not the president and we lose our current trustees, we will never be able to pass a bond." The interim president indicates that she will need to bring this problem to the attention of the trustees at their meeting the following week. The VPI feels that it is important to complete the investigation into the allegations of misallocation of work-study and travel funds and falsification of financial documents that the investigator brought to his attention. He tells the interim president that the athletic conference commissioner is expecting a full report on any findings of recruitment violations. The interim president tells the VPI, "Call the commissioner and tell him that after a thorough investigation we did not find any substantial violations and that the president has closed the case." The VPI protests, but the interim president reiterates the importance of getting the trustees reelected and a facilities bond passed. She tells him that he and the dean are not to disclose any information about potential misallocation of funds, falsification of documents, or fraudulent behavior on the part of the coach. She also tells him, "The only thing we are going to tell the trustees and the public is that the coach has been caught violating the athletic commission's recruitment rules." She then informs the VPI of her plan to ask the trustees to take action to dismiss the coach based on his recruitment activities. Finally, she calls the college's attorney and requests that formal dismissal papers be drafted for her and the board chair to sign.

Questions

Put yourself in the VPI's position and consider the following questions:

- How would you handle this situation with the athletic commission and coach?
- What would your response be to the president? What are potential ramifications for following or not following the president's direct orders?
- What are the ramifications of this case for the student athletes, the college's reputation, and the local community?

Part II: When Troubles Just Keep Getting Worse: The Missteps of Two Senior Administrators in Handling Problems With a Basketball Coach

Continuation of the Case

The VPI calls the commissioner to tell him that the investigator did not find any substantial rule violations and that the interim president has "closed the case." After a long pause, the commissioner calmly indicates that he obtained a copy of the investigator's report from an anonymous source, and that the case is far from being "closed." The commissioner expresses anger at the VPI's dishonesty and demands that either the college president place the team on disciplinary probation or he will, and that the team must forfeit all of its games over the past two years including the regional championship it won. The commissioner states that the college must also report the financial aid and other egregious violations to the local authorities and the federal government. He threatens to permanently bar the coach from coaching but says he will talk directly to the interim president before taking any such action. The commissioner then says that he is giving the college 10 days to take action against the coach and the basketball program.

The interim president briefs the trustees about the basketball coach's recruitment violations and recommends that they begin the process of firing him. Because the coach is a tenured faculty member, a dismissal hearing will be scheduled. She also tells the trustees that it is unlikely that the faculty union will provide support for the coach because, in her words, "The union leadership is made up of academic types who don't see much value in athletics." She also knows that the faculty union is struggling financially and surmises that it will not want to spend its limited resources on a costly fight over a coach. A number of the trustees express concern about the possibility of negative publicity, because the college's basketball program has been so popular. The interim president instructs the VPI to meet with the coach and give him a letter she has signed placing the coach on administrative leave with the intent to move toward termination.

On returning to his office, the VPI is confronted by the president of the faculty union about plans to fire the coach. The VPI is shocked because the only individuals who should have knowledge of the personnel action are the seven trustees, the president, and himself. The union president indicates that the accusations are false and that the union will fight against the firing of the coach. The VPI later gives the coach the letter from the interim president. The VPI tells the coach that he would be better off resigning and finding a new position at a different college. Then the VPI reports to the interim president that it appears that the union and the coach will fight the termination, and that the college needs to include the issues of embezzlement, fraud, and theft as reasons for termination. The interim president directs the VPI to begin preparing for the dismissal hearings and tells him that she and the board of trustees want the dismissal to move quickly and without a lot of fanfare. She also reminds him that the trustees do not know anything about the "money issues" and says that she has no intention of telling them about them. The interim president once again expresses her anger at the VPI for not informing her sooner about the problems with the coach. She states that if the way he handled this situation ends up jeopardizing her chances of becoming the permanent president, or if it causes undue political and election problems for any of the trustee members, he can plan on looking for a new job.

The college's attorney drafts and files the proper personnel documents to begin the dismissal process. The official justification is based on the dishonesty and unsatisfactory performance of the coach in conducting his duties. The recruitment violations are the only reason given on the dismissal documents; no mention is made of the coach's falsifying payroll and travel reimbursement forms or taking money from the basketball players. Based on previous experience with personnel matters, the VPI knows that in a faculty termination hearing the only evidence that can be brought against the coach is what is stated in the dismissal documents. Therefore, the only grounds for firing the coach are recruitment violations; the other more serious problems can not be presented during the hearing. The VPI has grave concerns that the hearing officer will not view the recruitment violations as adequate grounds for termination, and if the VPI tries to bring up the other issues, the union's attorney will quickly object and stop the evidence from being considered.

The next day, the VPI is awakened at 6:00 a.m. by a phone call from a sports reporter at the local newspaper. The reporter tells him that he received a message the previous night that the college has fired the coach and is going to terminate the basketball program. The VPI responds that he can not discuss personnel matters but offers that the college has been conducting a review of all the athletic programs for compliance with athletic commission regulations. The reporter then asks whether there are any major problems with the basketball program and, if so, whether the college would consider terminating the program. The VPI indicates that if there were serious enough problems, there are a number of actions the college might consider. The reporter then asks "hypothetically" if one of those options might be to terminate the program, and the VPI replies noncommittally, "I suppose it may be an unlikely option."

That afternoon the headline on the front page of the local newspaper reads, "College Officials Fire Coach and Are Likely to Dump Basketball Program." The article states that the college, acting on "rumors" of recruitment violations, abruptly fired the coach and is seriously considering closing the basketball program. The article also quotes the faculty union president as stating that the interim president is using this matter as an excuse to get rid of the men's sports program. Prominent local basketball supporters also are quoted as saying that the coach is an honest man and that the interim president and trustees are just angry that the basketball team will not make the conference playoffs. The article goes on to misquote the VPI, saying that the college is looking into closing its entire athletic program. The article prompts a strong public outcry and debate throughout the community, and numerous letters to the editor calling for the interim president to be fired and the trustees to resign.

After three weeks of public criticism and outcry, the VPI sits in his office contemplating what to do about this mess that just will not go away. He realizes that the sequence of actions both he and the interim president took, and the decisions they made, caused the whole situation to blow up into a public relations and personnel nightmare. He identifies the following options: (a) he can start looking for a new job, (b) he can focus on preparing the best case possible for termination of the coach despite the limitations of the evidence he can present to the hearing officer, or (c) he can take the evidence of the coach's criminal behavior directly to the local law enforcement authorities. The latter option is particularly appealing because of the new "whistle-blower" state law, which means that he can not be fired for disclosing criminal behavior to the local authorities. However, such a disclosure could lead to the loss of federal financial aid funds, and the college could be required to pay back to the federal government the thousands of dollars in financial aid that it has received.

Questions

- What actions should have been taken by the VPI and the dean early on in this case to help avoid the disastrous outcomes?
- Was the VPI justified in trying to manage the problems with the basketball program on his own at first without informing the interim president?
- Why did both the interim president and trustees underestimate the public backlash of firing the coach? How could the public relations issues have been managed better?
- How did the interim president's ambitions of becoming the permanent president and getting the trustees reelected and passing a facilities bond shape the way that she initially approached this problem and her actions throughout this case? How did she justify her actions in terms of trying to benefit the college?
- Is it ever acceptable for leaders to withhold information about potentially serious problems from the trustees (for presidents), or their supervisors (for other leaders), especially information regarding likely criminal behavior of an employee?

Nevarez & Wood–Situational Leadership Inventory (NW-SLI)

This leadership inventory is designed to aid leaders in assessing their usage of situational leadership theory. Current leaders should reflect on actions that they typically take and perceptions that they hold. Aspiring leaders should consider the actions that they would take if they held a formal leadership position within an organization. Read the following statements and mark the appropriate response. If you find statements difficult to answer, trust your instinct and judgement in selecting the most appropriate for you. Remember that there are no right or wrong answers. Key: 1 = Strongly Disagree, 2 = Disagree, 3 = Somewhat Disagree, 4 = Somewhat Agree, 5 = Agree, and 6 = Strongly Agree.

	Strongly Disagree	Disagree	Somewhat Disagree	Somewhat Agree	Agree	Strongly Agree
1. I am cognizant of the degree of authority between myself and my staff						
2. I always consider the social landscape of my organization before making any decision						
3. Effective decisions necessitate having a full understanding of a problem						
4. I frequently assess employees' willingness to complete tasks before determining my leadership approach						
5. I am aware of the power balance between leaders and followers in my organization						
6. Leaders must understand the relationship between themselves and followers before making any decision						
7. I always make sure I understand a problem fully before trying to fix it						
8. I frequently gauge employees' ability level before determining my leadership approach						

9. Effective leaders understand the power differential between themselves and their staff						
10. Leaders who understand workplace relationships will make the most effective decisions						
11. I explore various alternatives to addressing the task at hand						
12. I believe the best results are achieved by understanding staff members' motivation						
13. The leadership style employed by a leader is dependent upon the level of authority between leaders and staff						
14. I attempt to engage in positive interactions with all employees in efforts to develop a friendly workplace environment						
15. Leaders should always know the intricacies of a problem before trying to address it						
16. I believe the best results are achieved by understanding staff members' competencies						

Scoring

Situational theory leaders are known for using a multiplicity of strategies and approaches to reach their end goals. They believe that there tends to be a "best" approach among many approaches to take in a given situation. To score your responses, add your responses to all of the statements in the inventory. This is your total situation leadership score. Higher scores indicate greater levels of situational theory usage, whereas lower scores indicate lower levels of usage. The maximum score possible is 96.

_____ Total Situational Leadership Score

To better understand how your score relates to the primary components of situational leadership, (a) add your responses to statements 1, 2, 5, 6, 9, 10, 13, and 14 (this is your total degree of authority score); (b) add your responses to statements 3, 7, 11, and 15, and then multiply the sum by 2 (this is your total understanding the task score); and (c) add your responses to statements 4, 8, 12, and 16, and then multiply the sum by 2 (this is your total level of maturity score). The maximum score for each subscale is 48.

_____ Degree of Authority _____ Understanding the Task

_____ Level of Maturity

Definitions

Degree of Authority. This refers to the amount of authority a leader has over followers. A subcomponent of this authority is leader-member relations, that is, the climate and culture of the work environment as influenced by the relationship between the leader and employee. This is inclusive of the degree of admiration, respect, and confidence that followers have for the organizational leader.

Understanding the Task. This refers to the leader's understanding, assessment, and evaluation of a task as well as the path to addressing the task.

Level of Maturity. This refers to the leader's assessment of staff members' motivation and level of ability.

Score Meaning

While the maximum score is 96 total and 48 for each subscale, many leaders may desire to understand their usage of this framework in comparison with that of other leaders. To facilitate this interest, scores from prior inventory participants were divided into percentile ranges. These percentile ranges allow leaders to understand their score in relation to the scores of other leaders. The percentile ranges are as follows: Low situational orientation (25th percentile or lower), Medium situational orientation (26th to 50th percentile), High situational orientation (51st to 75th percentile), and Very High situational orientation (76th to 99th percentile)

- Low situational orientation: 60–74 points
- Medium situational orientation: 75–79 points
- High situational orientation: 80–84 points
- Very High situational orientation: 85–96 points

Subscales can be interpreted simplistically as low scores and high scores. Based on scores from previous participants, scores of 39 or below are low subscale scores and scores of 40 or greater represent high adherence to the subelements (i.e., degree of authority, understanding the task, and level of maturity).

Improve Your Situational Leadership Score

Assessment of the Situation. Develop the skills to evaluate any given situation from multiple perspectives taking into account contextual information surrounding respective situations. In doing so, you will facilitate your understanding of the best course of action.

Relationship Building. Think of multiple ways in which you can develop positive relationships. Facilitate the development of formal (e.g., workshops, meetings, seminars) and informal (e.g., lunch, coffee talks) events that foster contact among personnel. Understanding social interactions within the organization will better allow you to determine which leadership approach is needed in any given situation.

Motivation. Pay particular attention to what motivates people in the organization and develop the skills to motivate high-ability and low-ability individuals. For example, some individuals are motivated by the assignment of complex tasks, others by salary increases, and yet others by flexible work hours.

Multidimensional Leadership Approach. Learn to have an astute awareness of multiple leadership theories and approaches. A monostyle approach to leadership will not work in addressing the complex nature of social organizations.

Reliability

Two internal consistency estimates were employed to examine the reliability of the overall contingency-situation leadership inventory: split-half coefficient and coefficient alpha. For the split-half reliability, the scale was divided into equal halves for item equivalency. We took into account the order of the measures; thus, the sequence of items was rotated. One half consisted of items 1, 3, 5, 7, 9, 11, 13, and 15 and the other half consisted of items 2, 4, 6, 8, 10, 12, 14, and 16. The split-half coefficient was .84 and the coefficient alpha was .88. Both procedures illustrated satisfactory reliability. The following coefficient alphas are associated with each subconstruct: .75 (degree of authority), .79 (understanding the task), and .74 (level of maturity). To view this inventory or learn more about using the inventory for research purposes, see http://communitycollegeleadership.net.

Suggested Reading

Nevarez, C., & Wood, J. L. (2011). *Nevarez & Wood–Situational Leadership Inventory (NW-SLI)*. Sacramento, CA: Nevarez-Wood Community College Leadership Institute.

7

ETHICAL LEADERSHIP

Ethics and morality are two concepts that are often used to refer to an individual's pursuit of "right" or "good" courses of action. In general, scholars delineate between the two concepts, noting that *ethics* refers to an established standard of good while *morality* is the process of carrying out that standard. In the context of leadership, the terms *ethical leadership* and *moral leadership* are used interchangeably to refer to employing right actions when leading others. In general, several (sometimes competing) metatheories of applied ethics are used to determine whether actions enacted by leaders meet an established standard of good; these metatheories consist of deontology, teleology, and axiology (Beckner, 2004; Northouse, 2007). Within each of these metatheories are multiple subtheories, which provide additional guidance in pursuing good problem resolution. Although there are similarities in these theories (i.e., "doing the right thing," terminology used), there is wide variation in how these similar concepts are approached, understood, and defined.

Deontology connotes that the best action is not a by-product of its outcome, but the mechanisms by which the outcome is sought (Gaus, 2001). Deontology has been referred to as means-based and nonconsequentialist thinking (to connote that the consequences of an action are not considered) (Beckner, 2004; van Staveren, 2007). Essentially, these terms suggest that leaders' concern should focus on the methods and mechanisms by which their decisions are made as opposed to the end (outcomes) of a given decision. One type of deontology is referred to as the ethic of justice. This theory suggests that decisions should be based solely on existing rules, codes, policies, and laws (Delgado, 1995; Maxcy, 2002; Strike, Haller, & Soltis, 2005). An example of this deontological approach would be a community college leader who makes decisions based solely on the rules in place (e.g., institutional policies) without taking into account the outcomes produced by those rules or contextual factors that may perpetuate inequalities. While deontologists hope for good outcomes, they believe that having "objective" rules or principles is more important. When rules exist that serve to create outcomes that are unjust, the leader works to change those rules through the proper structures and mechanisms in place, while still enforcing the rules until they are formally changed (Shapiro & Gross, 2008; Shapiro & Stefkovich, 2005).

Whereas deontology is focused on the *means* by which a decision is made, teleology is concerned with the *ends* of a given decision. Thus, *teleology* is referred to as *ends-based, outcome-focused,* and *consequentialist thinking* (Beckner, 2004). In all, these terms indicate that when someone is faced with an issue or a dilemma, the appropriate decision is one that promotes the best end result or outcome. In this light, leaders are not so much concerned with the action used to obtain a desired end (e.g., student persistence, articulation agreements, fund-raising); on the contrary, their attention is given to the end result, producing the best possible outcome. The idea of what the best outcome is in any given situation is the primary point of departure in teleological theories. Some experts suggest that the most effective outcome is one that promotes the best interest of the decision maker (Avolio & Locke, 2002; Smith, 2006). This theory, referred to as egoism, suggests that the primary concern of leaders should be *their* advancement, *their* power, *their* development, and *their* careers. While extreme egoism would likely produce negative results for community colleges (most notably by taking the focus away from students), many would agree that a healthy focus on oneself is necessary. Utilitarianism is another primary teleological theory, which is juxtaposed to egoism. This theory suggests that the most effective course of action is one that produces the greatest good for the greatest number of people (students, faculty, community). These theories are both teleological, in that the outcome (e.g., the best end result for oneself or the greater community) is the focus of the ethical practice. Utilitarianism focuses on how decisions affect others and places the benefits to and interests of society above those of individuals (Beckner, 2004; van Staveren, 2007).

However, the scope of what constitutes the group for which leaders should advocate this "greatest good" can be uncertain. Wider society could easily refer to a number of differing groups (e.g., world, nation, state, region, county). To address this concern, the ethic of local community has been espoused as an ethical lens for community college leaders. This ethic operates from a utilitarian and communitarian frame; it is a belief that the local community should be placed in the center of decision making. More specifically, it delimits the greatest good to the service region of the community college. In this light, the best course of action for a given community college is one that addresses the best interests (e.g., economic, social, political) of the local community as pursued through academic programming. This perspective suggests a reductionist view of each college's respective mission (e.g., comprehensive educational programming, open access, lifelong learning) and functions (e.g., transfer, terminal degrees, remedial education). Leaders operating from this perspective focus on obtaining excellence in a more limited number of areas that are most important to the vitality of the local community as a whole. Thus, the needs of the community shape the foci of the institutions that serve the community. This perspective is rooted in the historical orientation of "community" colleges as institutions designed to serve the needs of their local communities through academic programming.

Another popular subtheory among teleologists is the ethic of critique. The ethic of critique is critical of an ethic of justice approach. Rooted in a philosophy similar to that of critical theory, it suggests that rules, laws, and codes are created by the powerful to maintain their power and to subjugate the powerless (Caldwell, Shapiro, & Gross, 2007; Nevarez & Wood, 2010). Thus, this perspective sees rule-based decision making as blind to how rules hurt others, particularly the underprivileged. Leaders employing the ethic of critique frame are often guided by their desire to create equity, social justice, and advocate for the marginalized. They raise concerns over how policies are made, by whom they are made, the reason for their enactment, whom they will benefit, and whom they will disadvantage. In all, these leaders believe that the right course of action is one that promotes parity, deconstructs oppressive structures, and resists systems of marginalization.

Axiology is another ethical metatheory. *Axiology* is the Greek word for "value," and as such, axiology is also referred to as value theory. However, axiology is more concerned with virtues than values (Beckner, 2004). Values are concepts and characteristics that are *valued*, or important. For example, community college leaders may value beautiful facilities, close proximity to lunchtime eateries, and inexpensive parking. However, the reduction of these values would not lead to imminent organizational quandaries. In contrast to values, virtues are characteristics and concepts for which leaders and their organizations cannot do without; they are *highly* esteemed values. Common examples of virtues are justice, equity, honesty, and integrity. These virtues are highly esteemed in that college subunits, students, and the local communities served by community colleges would be adversely impacted by their absence.

From an axiological perspective, every profession (e.g., faculty, counseling, student services) is guided by a set of virtues that should serve to facilitate decision making. In the community college, there are a number of virtues that should be in play. The importance of certain virtues will often depend on contextual factors within the institution and the communities that it serves. There are several virtues that are directly applicable to leadership in the community college: diversity, community, honesty, and prudence (sound judgment). Using these virtues, community college leaders encountering issues would decide that the best course of action is one that maximizes these virtues. Thus, it is assumed that the propagation of these virtues themselves is, in fact, "good" leadership.

An additional type of axiological theory is the ethic of care. The ethic of care asserts that the greatest virtues are compassion, caring, understanding, trust, and otherness (Gilligan, 1982; Noddings, 2003). Given the importance of having balance between otherness and personal well-being, classic literature on the ethic of care has employed a three-stage process of understanding how individuals use this lens. In the first stage, individuals are solely focused on their own needs (akin to egoism), with the motivation guiding their self-interest focused on avoiding harm from others. In the second stage, individuals become fully altruistic. They focus their efforts *completely* on the well-being, interests, and concerns of others, even to the point of their own detriment. In the third stage, individuals develop a balance between the needs of others and their own needs, realizing that healthy relationships necessitate mutual respect and connectivity. In the community college, leaders employing an ethic of care frame often focus their efforts on building community, forming bonds, and being attentive to the needs of others. They believe that doing so will facilitate the "right" course of action in any given situation (Pratt, Skoe, & Arnold, 2004; Skoe, 2010; Skoe, Cumberland, Eisenberg, Hansen, & Perry, 2002; Skoe & Marcia, 1991).

Discussion Questions

Consider the following questions in your analysis of the leadership theory presented in this chapter. In addition, pose your own analytical questions that will aid you in better articulating, analyzing, and critiquing the intricacies of this leadership theory.

- What are the strengths and limitations of the ethical theories presented in this chapter?
- How does the relationship between the leader and the follower differ for each of the theories presented?
- How is influence gained, maintained, and extended in each theory?
- How can ethical leaders inform the resolution of critical issues faced by community college leaders?
- In what ways have you seen an ethical leadership paradigm employed within your organizational setting?
- How does your preferred leadership style compare to the ethical leadership theories in this chapter?
- In what ways (if any) could your personal leadership be enhanced by ethical theories?
- In what way do the ethical theories discussed in this chapter compare with and differ from other leadership theories presented in this book?

Francisco Rodriguez
President/Superintendent
MiraCosta Community College

A Grade-Changing Scandal

Background

Jared McIntire is a newly hired dean of enrollment and records at Charity Mountain Community College (CMCC). Jared has worked in admissions and records offices for more than 20 years, with experience in several community colleges. He started his career as a student assistant and worked his way up through the ranks. However, this is his first post as dean. This is an opportunity to operate his *own* admissions and records office. Jared uprooted his family from their East Coast networks, family, and friends for a new life in the northwestern United States. Although the institution provided funding to cover some moving costs, the move has placed the McIntire family in a financial hole, one that should be remedied within the next nine months. Jared will be assuming leadership over a staff of 20 full-time staff and 10 student workers. The team is quite small given the range of responsibilities covered by his department (e.g., outreach, admissions, testing, orientation, records). However, given his extensive experience, Jared believes that he can effectively lead this team.

CMCC is not particularly diverse with most of the student body composed of White students (89%) and the remainder representative of multiple racial/ethnic groups (Native Americans, Latinos, and a handful of African Americans). Upon being hired at CMCC, Jared was ecstatic. The college is nationally renowned as a leader in student success, boasting an 85% certificate and associate's degree completion rate and a 74% transfer rate. College leaders from around the country come to learn about the "great work" that is being done at CMCC. In particular, a recent report released by the National Science Foundation has hailed CMCC as a model institution for its success in facilitating the preparation and transfer of science and math majors. The report has been widely distributed, resulting in increased philanthropic donations for a new science, engineering, technology, and mathematics center. The institution is also a finalist for a large grant from the U.S. Department of Education that would provide the remaining funds needed for the construction of the science center. In addition, the report has come to the attention of several national news networks, resulting in CMCC being featured on education specials by CNN, MSNBC, and Fox News. Furthermore, the National Aeronautics and Space Administration has recently selected five CMCC students to participate in its National Community College Aerospace Scholars program. Given CMCC's reputation, political leaders at the local, state, and even national level often visit the campus and cite it as a model for "best practices."

Statement of the Problem

At the end of his first semester, Jared is pleased with the success of his team. Though quite small (considering the large enrollment at CMCC), the team has developed new policies and processes that have increased efficiency. Jared believes in sharing the credit for a job well done and has regularly told his administrative colleagues about the fine efforts of the full-time staff and student workers whom he supervises. Late one evening, Jared drives to the office to work on a presentation that he is giving to a local community organization. He does not normally do late-night work on campus, but his family is out of town visiting relatives, so he feels there is no sense in working from home. As he walks up to his admissions and records office, he can see light underneath the door and hears whispering coming from the office. He recognizes the voices of two of his student assistants. One of them says, "Did you finish changing the grades yet? We gotta get out of here. I still can't believe she gives you her access code for this!" Then the other responds, "Almost there, relax. . . . I'm tellin' you, I'm a pro at this. I've been doing this for a long time . . . and . . . don't worry, I definitely make it worth her while." Jared is shocked and bewildered by the nature of the conversation. Fearful of how the student assistants might react if confronted, he turns around, leaves the building, returns to his car, and drives home.

At home, Jared's mind races—he does not sleep at all. He returns to work early in the morning and runs a special analysis that identifies all grades that have been changed within the past 12 hours. He finds 40 questionable changes that do not have faculty verification; all of these grades were changed with an access code belonging to Susan, a full-time employee in the office. From what Jared knows of her, she began working in the office as a student assistant and as a result of her exemplary work was hired after she earned her associate's degree. Remembering that one of the students mentioned that he had been making changes for a long time, Jared checks the records on past semesters. He identifies approximately 300 grade changes over the past two years that lacked full documentation. All of these changes were made with Susan's access code. The more Jared delves into the data, the more he realizes that most (but not all) of the changes were made for students in the sciences.

Distressed by this discovery and concerned about the possibility of losing his position, Jared makes a phone call to his longtime mentor Dan, a retired vice president of student services from the East Coast institution where Jared previously worked. Dan and Jared have a very strong friendship; he knows that Dan is the only person he can fully trust with such a sensitive situation. He recounts the entire ordeal to Dan, who is understandably shocked by the gravity of the situation. Dan tells Jared of a similar situation that occurred at Diablo Valley Community College in California in which nearly 400 grades had been changed in exchange for cash payments and in some cases sexual favors. He notes that administrators lost their jobs and that the local community is still reeling from the effects of the scandal.

Dan asks Jared if he has told anyone else at his institution about the situation, and Jared assures him that he has not. Dan tells Jared that he would not be surprised if this is the reason that Jared's predecessor left the post. He outlines the likely ramifications of the grade-changing scheme coming to light, noting that the institution's reputation would be deeply marred, jeopardizing current and future private and federal funding and leading to investigations by local and national teams. Dan notes that the outcome would be devastating for CMCC alumni, current students, and the local community served by the institution. He also states that given the length of time that the grade-changing has been occurring, there will inevitably be problems with multiple institutions because any student who has had an illegitimate grade change and then transferred those course credits to another community college or four-year institution will have involved those institutions in the scandal. Dan informs Jared that CMCC's human resources policy will undoubtedly have a mandated reporting requirement for fraudulent behavior. He suggests that Jared look up his institution's policies relevant to this matter.

With all this in mind, Dan tells Jared that he sees only three viable options in this situation. He notes that the options are not mutually exclusive and that they represent only his initial thoughts. The first option is that Jared could report the situation—send it up the ladder through the administrative ranks. The benefit of doing so would be shifting the burden of determining the right course of action to those at the executive level. Dan notes

that this is the most responsible and ethical course of action but that Jared
will be an easy scapegoat. After all, his student workers and at least one of
his staff members are responsible. As their supervisor, Jared is, by default,
responsible for their actions—regardless of whether he hired them or knew
about the grade-changing scheme. As a result, Dan believes that Jared likely
will be fired. He states that with a problem of this magnitude, other administrative heads will roll as well. Jared tells Dan that he is just now starting to
get out of a financial hole and can not afford to lose his job. Dan tells Jared
that this is likely the least of his worries, that this circumstance will forever
mar his professional reputation, and he will likely have trouble finding
another job in higher education.

Then Dan presents a second option. Jared could keep the problem to
himself, handle it on his own, and never tell anyone. He tells Jared that he
could go back and rechange the altered grades from the past semester. That
would mean that only those grades from the time his predecessor was in the
post would still be questionable. He notes that this would likely remove *some*
of the burden from him, but not all. Dan notes that he could document
poor performance on Susan's part in the next several months. He could give
her successive write-ups for minor issues and either hope that she leaves or,
if needed, use the performance paper trail to eliminate her. Dan points out
that this could bury the situation but that he would always have to worry
about the scandal coming to light because someone would eventually talk.
He tells Jared, "It's not a matter of *if* someone finds out but *when*. How you
handle it will determine the impact it will have on you." He cautions that
an in-depth investigation could uncover that Jared did not report the problem and only changed the grades for which he was responsible. The third
option Dan presents is for Jared to pretend that he knows nothing about the
grade changes, leave all the grades as they stand, and apply *immediately* to
another position at another institution, even if it means a small step back in
title and pay. Finally, Dan notes that he has an old friend who is a retired
college counsel and suggests that Jared consider following up with him to
understand the legal ramifications of the situation.

Questions

In this scenario, assume that you are Jared. You can either choose one of
Dan's options, choose a mix of his options, or come up with your own

approach. When contemplating what you will do, consider the following questions:

- What ramifications could this situation have for the campus?
- What is the best interest for Jared? His family? His career?
- What outcome would create the best outcome for the local community?
- What would normal protocol and policies suggest that Jared do? What would likely be the outcome for the students? For Susan, the staff member? For Jared? For members of the campus administration?

Nevarez & Wood–Ethical Leadership Inventory (NW-ELI)

This leadership inventory is designed to aid leaders in assessing their usage of ethical leadership theory. Ethical leaders strive to make the "right" decisions; however, the method(s) of reaching the "right" decision depends on the ethical frame. While there are a number of differing ethical paradigms, this inventory focuses on three theories key to leadership in the community college: the ethic of justice, the ethic of critique, and the ethic of care. Current leaders should reflect on actions that they typically take and perceptions that they hold. Aspiring leaders should consider the actions that they would take if they held a formal leadership position within an organization. Read the following statements and mark the appropriate response. If you find statements difficult to answer, trust your instinct and judgement in selecting the most appropriate for you. Remember that there are no right or wrong answers. Key: 1 = Strongly Disagree, 2 = Disagree, 3 = Somewhat Disagree, 4 = Somewhat Agree, 5 = Agree, and 6 = Strongly Agree.

	Strongly Disagree	Disagree	Somewhat Disagree	Somewhat Agree	Agree	Strongly Agree
1. Having strong rules, policies, and procedures will always lead to better organizational outcomes						
2. Rules and policies often create unintended consequences for the disadvantaged						
3. Care and compassion typify my leadership style						
4. Advocating for individuals not at the "decision-making table" is my top priority						
5. Leaders should always adhere to the rules and regulations in place						
6. Social structures and the rules that support them perpetuate stratification						
7. Creating a sense of community at work is an ethical imperative						

8. I always consider how policies can disadvantage others						
9. Following a policy is more important than the outcome of the policy						
10. Sometimes, you must ignore policies to do what is "right"						
11. My chief concern is the well-being and welfare of my staff						
12. In all cases, the "right" thing to do is to follow the rules, policies, and protocols in place						
13. Workplace relationships must be typified by trust and understanding						
14. To be effective, a leader must care about and affirm their staff						
15. I establish codes and policies for my staff and expect them to be followed at all times						

Note. This inventory is printed with permission from the Nevarez-Wood Community College Leadership Institute. All rights reserved.

Scoring

Three types of ethical leadership are addressed in this inventory: the ethic of justice, the ethic of critique, and the ethic of care. To better understand how your score relates to these ethical frames, (a) add your responses to statements 1, 5, 9, 12, and 15 (this is your total ethic of justice score); (b) add your responses to statements 2, 4, 6, 8, and 10 (this is your total ethic of critique score); and (c) add your responses to statements 3, 7, 11, 13, and 14 (this is your total ethic of care score). The maximum score for each subscale is 30.

____ Ethic of Justice   ____ Ethic of Critique   ____ Ethic of Care

Definitions

> *Ethic of Justice.* The leader believes the "right" course of action is associated with upholding rules, laws, codes, policies, and regulations, regardless of the outcome or consequence.

Ethic of Critique. The leader believes that the rules, laws, and codes are created by the powerful to maintain their power and subjugate the powerless.

Ethic of Care. The leader believes that the "right" action will demonstrate virtues of compassion, love, care, and connectedness.

Score Meaning

While the maximum score for each subscale is 30, many leaders may desire to understand their usage of this framework in comparison with that of other leaders. To facilitate this interest, scores from prior inventory participants were divided into percentile ranges. These percentile ranges allow leaders to understand their score in relation to the scores of other leaders. The percentile ranges are as follows: Low orientation (33rd percentile or lower), Medium orientation (34th to 66th percentile), and High orientation (67th to 99th percentile).

Ethic of Justice	Ethic of Critique	Ethic of Care
Low justice orientation: 5–14 points	Low critique orientation: 5–22 points	Low critique orientation: 5–21 points
Medium justice orientation: 15–20 points	Medium critique orientation: 23–27 points	Medium critique orientation: 22–25 points
High justice orientation: 20–30 points	High critique orientation: 28–30 points	High critique orientation: 26–30 points

Improve Your Ethical Leadership Score

Ethic of Critique. Leaders are concerned with how rules and policies serve to further disadvantage the underserved. Identify faculty, staff, and student communities that are marginalized and make it a point to learn about their challenges. Be proactive in advocating for their issues, giving particular attention to organizational policies, rules, and procedures.

Ethic of Care. Leaders often focus their efforts on building community, forming bonds, and being attentive to the needs of others. Find opportunities to listen and build communities centered on developing a positive working environment. Be careful not to focus solely on the interests of others without attending to your own needs.

Ethic of Justice. Leaders make decisions from the perspective of "rule of law" and view laws as a need for sustaining civility and good of the community. Learn organizational rules, policies, and procedures. Have a better understanding of them in comparison with others around you. More important, know what is "written in stone" and what is not accounted for in policy. Use policy to gain control over others.

Reliability

The internal consistency of each construct was examined using coefficient alpha. The coefficient alpha for the ethic of justice was .78; the ethic of critique, .73; and the ethic of care, .75. These scales illustrated marginally satisfactory reliability. To view this inventory or learn more about using the inventory for research purposes, see http://communitycollegeleadership.net.

Suggested Reading

Nevarez, C., & Wood, J. L. (2011). *Nevarez & Wood–Ethical Leadership Inventory (NW-ELI)*. Sacramento, CA: Nevarez-Wood Community College Leadership Institute.

8

LEADER-MEMBER EXCHANGE THEORY

Leader-member exchange theory is grounded in the idea that leaders should strive to develop positive relationships with organizational affiliates through high-quality interactions between leaders and followers (Deluga, 1998; Pellegrini & Scandura, 2006). Leaders are encouraged to engage in positive interactions with each member of the organization (i.e., lower ranks, midmanagement, executives) irrespective of the employee's position; however, the leaders' approach will differ based on where the employee resides within the organizational structure. This theory also emphasizes linking the leadership style or approach to the affiliate's skill level, disposition, needs, and aspirations (Bauer & Green, 1996; Erdogan, Kraimer, & Liden, 2004; Liden, Sparrowe, & Wayne, 1997).

The philosophy driving leader-member exchange theory is that all organizational affiliates (e.g., groups, leaders, and employees) benefit from high-quality interactions. When these interactions take place, college employees benefit by feeling valued, a sense of belonging, and mutual trust and respect. As a result, an enhanced obligation to the organization ensues. The leader is better able to guide followers in achieving the organization's overall goals and objectives (e.g., comprehensive educational programming, student success) because of the formation of a positive mutual (dyad) relationship between the leader and the member (Graen & Uhl-Bien, 1995).

Once the positive relationship has been formed, based on positive interactions and employee willingness to take on additional responsibilities, organizational affiliates are symbolically welcomed to the "in-group." The in-group refers to the core of employees who are closest to the leader. Typically, employees considered to be part of an in-group are those whom the leader perceives to be well liked and trusted. This nucleus of loyalists forms a give-and-take relationship in which affiliates give more to the organization and in exchange receive the benefits of being core team members (Erdogan, Liden, & Kraimer, 2006; Liden & Maslyn, 1998). Ideally, leaders want all employees to be part of the in-group because the organization benefits from enhanced employee productivity and commitment; the leader benefits because of an enhanced work relationship with employees; and the employees benefit by having influence, power, better work schedules for followers, access to information and resources, negotiable roles and responsibilities, high-quality exchanges with the leader, and opportunities for advancement. While the benefits of being an in-group member are numerous, this membership carries with it a greater level of time commitment, loyalty, pressure, and expectations of exceeding contractual obligations.

Each employee is given (at some point) an opportunity to go beyond the call of duty and prove himself or herself worthy of being in the in-group. Employees' success and willingness to achieve beyond their contractual obligations and/or demonstration of loyalty to the leader or organization determines their in/out-group status (Dienesch & Liden, 1986; Graen & Uhl-Bien, 1995). Although some organizational affiliates are part of the in-group, many more are part of the out-group. There are several reasons why employees can become members of the out-group (e.g., lack of loyalty, incompetence, low success, limited skill level), but two are predominant. First, these followers do not share similar values, outlooks, dispositions, or working styles as the leader. The disconnect between out-group members and the leader ranges on a continuum from those who simply differ in style and approach to those who possess values, objectives, and visions differing from those of the leader. A perceived drawback of organizational affiliates being relegated to the out-group based on the perception of the leader is that leaders' perceptions can be flawed or informed by bias. Second, organizational affiliates are content with meeting their contractual obligations and nothing more. The work ethic often associated with members of the out-group includes taking all their breaks, vacation time, sick time, and family leave; adhering to the stated work hours as specified in their contract; and having a low degree of work productivity and efficiency (Gerstner & Day, 1997; Pellegrini, Scandura, & Jayaraman, 2010).

The differences between the in-group and out-group are evident within any organization. For example, a department head would offer a faculty member who is considered part of the in-group the opportunity to serve on a decision-making panel; whereas, an employee who is perceived to be associated with the out-group would not be afforded such an opportunity. It should be noted, however, that the degree to which a person is placed within either the in-group or out-group system is multidimensional. There are various layers and types of relationships between the leader and the employee that influence the degree to which the leader and employee engage and interact. This can also impact an employee's placement within an in-group or an out-group. Moreover, influence can be based on whether the employee is striving to persuade the leader to agree to a particular outcome (e.g., schedule, course selection) or whether the department head is using his or her power with faculty to adopt a particular methodology to ensure student success. In either case, the approach to gaining influence is governed by the interaction that exists between the leader and the employee.

As noted by Graen and Uhl-Bien (1995), the interaction between leaders and affiliates can be categorized into three primary stages. These stages are based on the roles, influences, exchanges, and interests of the leader and the employee as they relate to building a relationship. The development of the relationship between the leader and employee begins with the *stranger phase*. In this phase, the employee or leader is relatively new to the organization or post. Initially, the relationship is based on traditional autocratic style, in which the exchange is limited to the hierarchical status of the employee, and the subordinate is primarily motivated by self-interests (e.g., pay, benefits, schedule). Over time, the relationship shifts to the *acquaintance phase.* This phase is typically initiated when either the employee or the leader offers to share personal details, work-related information, or resources. This is a pivotal stage in the relationship-building process. It is the stage in which the employee decides whether he or she wishes to take on additional responsibilities and/or in which the leader determines whether to offer the employee additional professional challenges. The leader considers a number of factors when deciding whether the employee should be given more responsibility, including the employee's loyalty, whether the employee has been successful in fulfilling his or her responsibilities, the socioemotional intelligence and skill level of the employee, and the employee's ability to work effectively with other members of a team or with the leader. If the leader and employee are dissatisfied with the relationship in the second phase, the employee will refer back to the stranger phase. However, if they choose to continue to develop their relationship, they begin the transition to the third phase. In this stage, referred to as the *mature partner phase*, the leader and the employee begin to interact with one another on a greater level. Trust and respect are key components of this stage. The leader and employee engage in reciprocity, depending on each other for support in accomplishing organizational goals. The employee is no longer working solely from the perspective of self-interest; rather, there is reciprocal influence. Both parties trust each other, and both benefit from the positive relationship. Nevertheless, employee status as a mature partner is not necessarily fixed. Due to extenuating circumstances (e.g., health concerns, life stress, tenure, desire to reduce organizational commitment), the employee may opt to return to the stranger phase, where the pressures and demands are less strenuous.

Discussion Questions

Consider the following questions in your analysis of the leadership theory presented in this chapter. In addition, pose your own analytical questions that will aid you in better articulating, analyzing, and critiquing the intricacies of this leadership theory.

- What are the strengths and limitations of leader-member exchange theory?
- What is the relationship between the leader and the follower in leader-member exchange theory?
- How is influence gained, maintained, and extended in leader-member exchange theory?
- How can leader-member exchange leadership inform the resolution of critical issues faced by community college leaders?
- In what ways have you seen a leader-member exchange approach employed within your organizational setting?
- How does your preferred leadership style compare to a leader-member exchange leadership frame?
- In what ways (if any) could your personal leadership be enhanced by leader-member exchange theory?
- In what way does leader-member exchange leadership theory compare with and differ from other leadership theories presented in this book?

Carlos Nevarez and J. Luke Wood
California State University, Sacramento and
California State University, San Diego

Job Training for Whom?

Background

Northern City College (NCC) is a large community college serving a vibrant metropolitan area. The college is known for its commitment to diversity, equity, and social justice. This commitment is exemplified by programs that successfully incorporate college goers from varying racial/ethnic, gender, and socioeconomic groups. For instance, the institution has recently established several new vocational programs that provide unique career opportunities in naval (watercraft) engineering, airport operations, and transportation management, and staff are encouraged to recruit a broad base of applicants.

John is a new outreach advisor for NCC who is responsible for marketing and enrollment advising for adult reentry students. As a new employee, John will have a probationary hiring period of 90 days. Upon being hired, the director of the program pulled John aside and told him that he did everything to make sure John was selected, and his nonverbal gestures also subtly implied that John owed him.

John begins his position by working intensively with a number of community programs, organizations, and associations. There also is a partnership between the NCC and a nearby state prison to provide job training for released prisoners. Upon John's arrival at NCC, the director tells John that he is responsible for promoting the navel programs as well as increasing enrollment but does not give a formal sense of direction of how this is to be undertaken, nor does he provide any concrete end goals.

Given John's experience and background in program development, John approaches this task with excitement, confidence, and vision. As part of a new marketing effort for the naval engineering certificate program, John has begun a relationship with the state's prison release system. He gives weekly presentations to recently released prisoners. Enrollment in the program has drastically increased since John began marketing the program, primarily because the program is only nine months long, there is a high need for new workers in the field, and the pay is good. John believes his efforts are headed in the right direction, especially because the director of the program has even gone on outreach engagements with John to prison release meetings to advertise this program further.

Statement of the Problem

A week before courses start, John is pulled into an emergency meeting. Several academic deans and the dean of student services inform John that the director of the naval engineering program is unhappy. Apparently, due to the high volume of former inmates enrolling in naval engineering, the director is worried that his program will be branded negatively in the industry. He believes that this could result in difficulty finding jobs for all of his graduates. As a result, of the 60 students who were former inmates who had enrolled in the program, only five will be allowed to continue. The rest of the students will be encouraged to find a new program. In addition, campus officials have decided that because the students know John best, he will have to be the one to relay this information to them. Furthermore, to save face for the institution, John is told that the institution will inform the prison program that John, as a new employee, made a mistake in marketing and enrolling students in this specific program.

John is newly married and has small children; his house value is upside down because of the economic downturn; and there are continued family pressures for John, as the oldest son, to step up and support his ill parents. John struggles with how to proceed because he does not believe in what he is being asked to do but he can not afford to lose his job. Put yourself in John's shoes and consider the following questions:

- What are the conditions for workers under probationary status? Does the college have an "at will policy" that allows college administrators to terminate John's employment at any point during the probationary period?
- What are reasons for involving or not involving multiple stakeholders in addressing this situation?
- What alternative or additional approaches can be undertaken to support the enrollment of former inmates while addressing the concerns of the navel engineering certification program director?
- Whom should he reach out to for advice and support?
- What are John's options?

Nevarez & Wood–Leader-Member Exchange Theory Inventory (NW-LMETI)

This leadership inventory is designed to assess the degree to which a leader employs leader-member exchange theory. Current leaders should reflect on actions that they typically take and perceptions that they hold. For aspiring leaders, conceptualize how your actions in formal (e.g., work) and informal (e.g., home, extracurricular activities) settings may determine your degree of leader-member influence. Be sure to consider what your actions are, not what you would like them to be. Read the following statements and mark the appropriate response following your instinct; there are no right or wrong answers. Key: 1 = Strongly Disagree, 2 = Disagree, 3 = Somewhat Disagree, 4 = Somewhat Agree, 5 = Agree, and 6 = Strongly Agree.

	Strongly Disagree	Disagree	Somewhat Disagree	Somewhat Agree	Agree	Strongly Agree
1. I only invest myself in employees who "come through"						
2. I provide added benefits (preferential treatment) to employees who go beyond the "call of duty"						
3. There are some employees that I purposely avoid interaction with						
4. I am only committed to employees who are committed to me						
5. I am only loyal to employees who are loyal to me						
6. I have a core group of employees that I commit greater time to						
7. I have a core group of employees that I am loyal to						
8. I have a core group of employees with whom I have greater expectations						

9. I refrain from providing benefits to employees who do the bare minimum and/or do not meet my standards						
10. There are some employees I don't trust with information						

Scoring

To score your responses, add your responses to all of the statements in the inventory. This is your total leader-member exchange leadership score. Higher scores indicate greater levels of leader-member exchange orientation, whereas lower scores indicate lower levels of leader-member exchange orientation. The maximum score possible is 60.

_____ Total Leader-Member Exchange Score

Score Meaning

While the maximum score is 60, many leaders may desire to understand their usage of this framework in comparison with that of other leaders. To facilitate this interest, scores from prior inventory participants were divided into percentile ranges. These percentile ranges allow leaders to understand their score in relation to the scores of other leaders. The percentile ranges are as follows: Low leader-member exchange orientation (25th percentile or lower), Medium leader-member exchange orientation (26th to 50th percentile), High leader-member exchange orientation (51st to 75th percentile), and Very High leader-member exchange orientation (76th to 99th percentile).

- Low leader-member exchange orientation: 10–31 points
- Medium leader-member exchange orientation: 32–36 points
- High leader-member exchange orientation: 37–42 points
- Very High leader-member exchange orientation: 43–60 points

Improve Your Leader-Member Exchange Theory Score

Relationship Building. This theory is grounded on positive relationship building. Consider various ways in which you can establish and maintain positive relationships with people at all different levels of your institution. This requires not only being approachable, but seeking out opportunities to interact and engage with others.

Motivation. Try to identify ways in which people get motivated, and if you can, provide them to guide goal accomplishment. Be conscious of when individuals need to take on additional opportunities. Read articles on goal theory, motivation theory, and self-determination theory.

Opportunities for Growth. Know when individuals are prepared or want to move on to other opportunities and challenges, and be willing to support them. For those who are not ready to move on, provide them with incremental opportunities to improve their skills, knowledge, and abilities.

Emotional Intelligence. Leaders need to be able to gauge when individuals are ready for additional professional challenges and opportunities. To make this determination, it is important for leaders to consider individuals' loyalty, skill level, and ability to work well with others. Be reflective when talking with others, and be more attentive to what you are communicating through your body language and wording. In addition, try to better understand others' verbal and nonverbal communication.

Reliability

Two internal consistency estimates were employed to examine the reliability of the leader-member exchange theory leadership inventory: split-half coefficient and coefficient alpha. For the split-half reliability, the scale was divided into equal halves for item equivalency. We took into account the order of the measures; thus, the sequence of items was rotated. One half consisted of items 1, 3, 5, 7, and 9 and the other half consisted of items 2, 4, 6, 8, and 10. The split-half coefficient was .90 and the coefficient alpha was .83. Both procedures illustrated satisfactory reliability. To view this inventory or learn more about using the inventory for research purposes, see http://communitycollegeleadership.net.

Suggested Reading

Nevarez, C., & Wood, J. L. (2011). *Nevarez & Wood–Leader-Member Exchange Theory Inventory (NW-LMETI).* Sacramento, CA: Nevarez-Wood Community College Leadership Institute.

9

POLITICAL LEADERSHIP

P olitical leadership models are not based on static policies, practices, and regulations; rather, political leaders approach existing rules as an opportunity to renegotiate, modify, or create new processes in order to facilitate the short- and long-term goals of the leaders or their subunit (Hoy & Miskel, 2005). Negotiations are conducted through a process of interchanges that constitute continual give-and-take agreements among special-interest groups, power players, and coalitions. The leaders' varied interests and political affiliations lead to natural conflict, which is a by-product of the organizational groups' competing against each other for limited resources (Bolman & Deal, 2003). In the current era, many community colleges are experiencing financial turmoil, necessitating that programs and departments reduce their budgets. Under these circumstances, conflict arises among groups as they seek to sustain their services and operations in difficult budget climates. This problem is complicated by increased workloads, faculty/staff furloughs, growing student enrollment, and the reduction of resources. Thus, department heads must compete with one another to thrive, and in some cases survive.

In the case of political leaders, conflict is embraced and used to bargain and form coalitions to compete for power and resources. Consequently, the tendency is for political leaders to operate in a contentious work environment in which leaders use their political know-how to maneuver resources, people, and policies to advance goals (e.g., particularly subunit goals). During times of turmoil and crisis, political leaders use their power to configure the organization in a manner that advances their power. This can lead to the development of informal coalition building (Stoker, 1991, 1995).

93

There are several benefits to political leadership: (a) leaders can better advocate for the allocation of resources that maintain and enhance the vitality of their respective subunits and the institution; (b) leaders usually emerge around ideological standpoints; thus, these viewpoints compete and can contribute to positive organizational change; and (c) implementation of leaders' decisions is enhanced through networks of support, which can expedite their initiatives (Bass, 1985; Hoy & Miskel, 2005). Often, political leaders are concerned with institutionalizing beliefs and values that reinforce their influence and power. Politics are sometimes used to determine who will participate or be heard. The political leader is not necessarily concerned with how actions will impact the *entire* organization but, rather, how actions will benefit the leader personally, affect key issues currently being negotiated, leverage agendas for future negotiations, and serve to better advocate for the allocation of resources for the leader's subunit.

Political leaders are typified as highly critical thinkers as well as able to predict and envision others' actions and behaviors multiple steps in advance (Haus & Sweeting, 2006). Political leaders view leadership as a chess match, in that players are moved and positioned in a manner that allows for the greatest advantage over their opponent(s); there is an understanding that some players have greater worth, skill sets, and usability than others; and the players' ultimate goal is to outsmart their opponents and win "the game." This insight is obtained with an "any means necessary" philosophy. To anticipate behavior, leaders levy their networks, coalitions, and stakeholder groups; use pressure tactics; and negotiate resources, policies, and processes. Further, these leaders possess a high socioemotional intelligence and are able to understand the motivations, dispositions, and behaviors of others. These skills are critical for political leaders in that misjudgment could result in the loss of credibility, power, resources, and leverage. Such losses can negatively impact the subunits for which the leader advocates and serves. In realizing the implications of not succeeding, political leaders must be astute at predicting outcomes, behaviors, and actions of organization affiliates, particularly their adversaries. In addition, they must be knowledgeable of how external factors (e.g., policies, governing structures, political climate) will affect actions and the power balance within the institution. In all, political leaders are supported by the supposition that power is central to political success.

Power is also central to political theory. *Power* in general terms is defined as having the capacity to influence others through the use of authority (Yukl,

1989). Community college leaders hold power in that authority is bestowed on them by virtue of their being in formal positions. This authority grants them positional power, enabling them to persuade organizational affiliates' behaviors and drive the values of the institution. French and Raven (1959) identified five bases of power: legitimate, reward, coercive, expert, and referent. Political leaders are astute in these five forms of power.

Legitimate power is referred to as formal power provided by the organization for the purpose of allowing leaders to influence the direction of the institution. This form of power provides authority so that leaders can assert their influence over affiliate behavior in order to achieve organizational goals. For example, a department chair is often the formal authority over scheduling; although the chair may ask for input on the schedule, ultimately the decision resides with the chair.

Reward power can be considered a subset of legitimate power in that leaders in formal positions determine who in the organization is "worthy" of being granted a reward (e.g., promotion, recognition, perks, access to resources). This determination is based on what the leader perceives as desirable behaviors among followers. One example of reward power is when vice presidents promote entry-level staff to midlevel leadership based on their loyalty.

Coercive power is used to prevent or disadvantage individuals from obtaining certain goals through manipulation, punishment, and intimidation. This form of power dwells on the influence of threat or fear. Using this form of power typically requires leading in the margins of ethical and unethical practices. However, the focus of political leaders is not on the mechanism by which their end goal is sought, but the outcome itself. When taken to the extreme, this approach can create a toxic work environment. Community college leaders forcing faculty members to hire a new faculty member (or risk the safety of their own jobs) based on the leaders' relationship with the faculty applicant (e.g., the applicant is a family member of a college donor) would be one example of coercive power. Although this approach could delegitimize the equity of the hiring process, the financial outcome for an institution struggling on the margins of fiscal viability may be of greater importance.

Expert power refers to a leader's cognitive ability and a proven record of being an expert in a specialized area. This ability and expertise provide leaders with expert power because they are able to perform organizational tasks efficiently. Organizational affiliates trust expert leaders and pursue their input and guidance. A faculty member who is known as an instructional exemplar may be regarded by other faculty as an expert source on how to teach students effectively. As such, the faculty member may be sought out for advice, guidance, counsel, and mentorship in the area of teaching and learning.

Leaders with *referent power* are likable individuals because of their human relations approach. This approach is used to validate and empower others. These leaders are often seen as role models. This type of power is typically held by charismatic leaders, and power is accrued through the simple act of being likable. For example, a campus president who makes it a point to roam the halls and reach out to all constituents (e.g., faculty, staff, students) by being approachable, caring, and personable is viewed as exhibiting referent power. Often, college constituents make efforts to mimic the behavior of the leader because they admire and would like to posses such leader qualities.

Discussion Questions

Consider the following questions in your analysis of the leadership theory presented in this chapter. In addition, pose your own analytical questions that will aid you in better articulating, analyzing, and critiquing the intricacies of this leadership theory.

- What are the strengths and limitations of political theory?
- What is the relationship between the leader and the follower in political theory?
- How is influence gained, maintained, and extended in political theory?
- How can political leadership inform the resolution of critical issues faced by community college leaders?
- In what ways have you seen a political approach employed within your organizational setting?
- How does your preferred leadership style compare to a political leadership frame?
- In what ways (if any) could your personal leadership be enhanced by political theory?
- In what way does political leadership theory compare with and differ from other leadership theories presented in this book?

Edna V. Baehre
President
Central Pennsylvania's Community College

Power of Partnerships in Fund-Raising

Background

Since the 1990s, Harrisburg Area Community College (HACC), Central Pennsylvania's Community College, has had a history of fund-raising and having an enterprising and successful foundation. Currently, the HACC Foundation has a portfolio of more than $24.3 million. Each year, the foundation contributes more than $1.5 million to the college in scholarships, programs, facilities, and special initiative grants for faculty and staff support. Recently, the college received $3.5 million from three business leaders whose involvement with the college as a partner in workforce development led to the generous gifts. Two of the gifts are targeted for scholarships to students in high-demand technical and trade occupations, and one gift is to establish the Alex Grass Institute of Business Leadership at the college. The institute will include a unique leadership curriculum for the business administration programs and the development of a yearlong executive leadership academy to benefit midlevel managers who aspire to leadership positions.

The foundation has a long history of endowed funds. In fact, almost 90% of all donations are permanently restricted endowments, primarily for scholarships. However, in 2004, HACC and its foundation initiated its first capital campaign to raise $7.5 million (matched by $6 million in public funds from the Commonwealth of Pennsylvania) for a new health education pavilion and an early childhood education and licensed day care facility.

The college began planning for this capital campaign in early 2003 and kicked off the campaign in May 2004. The goal of $7 million in private funds was exceeded by half a million dollars within 18 months, and the buildings were opened by the fall of 2005. The very first donation, $1.2 million, setting the path for others to follow, came through a specialty hospital headquartered in the Harrisburg area. It was this first partnership that led to the realization that private/public partnerships tied to workforce and economic development was the avenue for this and future fund-raising efforts for the college. Through the partnership with the specialty hospital the college provided education and a limited number of customized training programs to hospital employees. The purpose of the first visit by the president and chair of the board was primarily to determine what else the college could do for the hospital to continue its success, not a direct solicitation. The president and chair informed the hospital president that they were in the process of expanding the health care education facilities but never mentioned the need to raise private dollars. As a follow-up to the visit to the hospital and under the direction of the college president, the college workforce training staff completed a comprehensive assessment of education and training needs for the hospital resulting in more customized training for 400-plus employees in medical coding and billing (free of charge to the hospital through a state grant that the college applied for on behalf of the hospital), and referral to credit programs for many employees for whom the hospital provided tuition support. Three months later the hospital committed to donate $1.2 million of $1.5 million. In every subsequent endeavor to obtain donations, the strategy was to approach an organization about what the college could do for its workforce. Through the use of this approach, more than 60% of the "asks" resulted in donations to support the capital campaign.

The college used the same strategy when it decided to concentrate all technical and trade degree programs by renovating an old 130,000-square-foot building in the urban area of Harrisburg. The goal was set at $3.5 million. The campaign kicked off in May 2007 and was completed in the late summer of 2008, with the goal surpassed by $100,000. Aside from exceeding the campaign goal in a downward economy, and in record time, there was an astonishing positive response rate of 94%. More than 100 businesses—from heating, ventilation, and air-conditioning contractors; to electrical contractors; to trade associations; to construction companies; to manufacturers; to plumbers; to architects; to engineering firms—provided capital donations to support the technical and trade programs in the business, recognizing readily that they would benefit from being able to tap into an educated and well-trained workforce after the students graduated.

Statement of the Problem

The college will be embarking on a $20 million capital campaign in the upcoming summer to expand its Public Safety Center (PSC) facilities using the same strategy of public/private partnerships tied to workforce development. A "PSC Partners" program has already raised more than $350,000 with $1,000 pledges over five years. The goal is to raise $1 million through 1,000 PSC Partners by the time the official campaign kicks off.

You are the newly appointed vice president for advancement who is working to build relationships with faculty, community leaders, and local business leaders. Within the community, there are some questions as to whether you are the right person for the job. Although you have held key leadership positions at the community college level for 20 years in large urban settings and are a visionary, your track record shows that your acquisition of external funding has been limited to federal grants. Moreover, some faculty and community members feel that the vice president of business affairs, who has been at the college since the last campaign, should have gotten the position. Clearly, your predecessor had a proven track record in raising funds to help drive the community college's mission; however, the economy has continued to falter, with many of the local businesses struggling to remain open. The president has provided you with the fund-raising campaign blueprint from the prior efforts as outlined in the previous section and expressed his confidence in you to get the job done. In preparation for the campaign, consider the following:

- How will you make a convincing case to the community to support the capital campaign?
- How can you leverage the partnerships with local businesses to secure donations for the capital campaign? How do you convince the business sector that the return on investment will easily be "paid back"?
- How will you establish a strategic campaign that uses volunteer support for making the case and the request for funds?
- How will you solicit strong financial support from college staff and faculty who have a vested interest in the capital campaign?
- How will you develop appropriate strategies for this campaign without having any prior experience in capital fund-raising?

Nevarez & Wood–Political Leadership Inventory (NW-PLI)

This leadership inventory is designed to assess the degree to which a leader adheres to a political frame. Current leaders should reflect on actions that they typically take and perceptions that they hold. For aspiring leaders, conceptualize how your actions in formal (e.g., work) and informal (e.g., home, extracurricular activities) settings may determine your degree of political influence. Be sure to consider what your actions are, not what you would like them to be. Read the following statements and mark the appropriate response following your instinct; there are no right or wrong answers. Key: 1 = Strongly Disagree, 2 = Disagree, 3 = Somewhat Disagree, 4 = Somewhat Agree, 5 = Agree, and 6 = Strongly Agree.

	Strongly Disagree	Disagree	Somewhat Disagree	Somewhat Agree	Agree	Strongly Agree
1. Leadership is akin to a game of "chess"						
2. I contemplate my actions multiple steps in advance						
3. I contemplate my opponents'/adversaries' actions multiple steps in advance						
4. I am a "power" player						
5. I know how to gain power over my opponents						
6. I maneuver people and resources to meet my goals						
7. I am adept in consolidating power						
8. I use the interests of my adversaries to gain advantage over them						
9. My actions are designed to position myself (and my sub-unit) for future battles						
10. I develop coalitions to gain power and resources						

Note. This inventory is printed with permission from the Nevarez-Wood Community College Leadership Institute. All rights reserved.

Scoring

To score your responses, add your responses to all of the statements in the inventory. This is your total political leadership score. Higher scores indicate greater levels of political orientation, whereas lower scores indicate lower levels of political orientation. The maximum score possible is 60.

_____ Total Political Leadership Score

Score Meaning

While the maximum score is 60, many leaders may desire to understand their usage of this framework in comparison with that of other leaders. To facilitate this interest, scores from prior inventory participants were divided into percentile ranges. These percentile ranges allow leaders to understand their score in relation to the scores of other leaders. The percentile ranges are as follows: Low political orientation (25th percentile or lower), Medium political orientation (26th to 50th percentile), High political orientation (51st to 75th percentile), and Very High political orientation (76th to 99th percentile).

- Low political orientation: 10–30 points
- Medium political orientation: 31–35 points
- High political orientation: 36–40 points
- Very High political orientation: 41–60 points

Improve Your Political Leadership Score

Conflict. Work toward being comfortable in dealing with conflict and, in doing so, use conflict to bargain and form coalitions to compete for resources and power.

Critical Thinking. Develop the skills to predict and envision barriers and opportunities for progress while identifying and aligning yourself with resources needed for your vision to be realized.

Coalition Building. Develop your human relations skills by expanding your network of acquaintances while promoting your ideas in a way that helps you develop coalitions centered on meeting your vision.

Goal Orientation. Be purposeful in setting goals, determining what re-sources will be needed to facilitate goal development, and establishing how your network of support can support goal attainment.

Reliability

Two internal consistency estimates were employed to examine the reliability of the political leadership inventory: split-half coefficient and coefficient alpha. For the split-half reliability, the scale was divided into equal halves for item equivalency. We took into account the order of the measures; thus, the sequence of items was rotated. One half consisted of items 1, 3, 5, 7, and 9 and the other half consisted of items 2, 4, 6, 8, and 10. The split-half coeffi-cient was .94 and the coefficient alpha was .92. Both procedures illustrated satisfactory reliability. To view this inventory or learn more about using the inventory for research purposes, see http://communitycollegeleadership.net.

Suggested Reading

Nevarez, C., & Wood, J. L. (2011). *Nevarez & Wood–Political Leadership Inventory (NW-PLI)*. Sacramento, CA: Nevarez-Wood Community College Leadership Institute.

10

SYSTEMS LEADERSHIP

S ystems leadership theory focuses on organizational behavior within the context of a system. We extend systems theory as derived from systems organizational theory, which concentrates on the importance of inputs, processes, outputs, and outcomes (Green, 2005, 2010). From an organizational standpoint, a system is described as an array of multiple, simple subparts (e.g., departments, units) that work within one larger and more complex whole (e.g., college). Systems have functions, operations, and policies, which are interrelated. These serve to connect the subsystems within the system or organization. Systems rely on each subpart to operate effectively and efficiently. The leader's primary role is to facilitate the linkage of multiple subsystems, enhance system efficiency through policies with increased organizational communication, and develop a clear strategic plan allowing multiple subsystems to work toward a unified goal. When each subunit operates at maximum capacity, it positively impacts the other subsystems within the larger system. For example, each department is, to some degree, affected by the status of other departments. As such, when one department does not operate effectively, the impact is felt throughout the system.

When a problem subsystem begins to affect other subsystems, each subsystem places pressure on the subsystem in question (Dooley, 1997; Swenson, 1991). This in turn produces several potential courses of action for the leader. First, the leader can enact policies, procedures, and interventions that force the subsystem in question to become more effective. For example, attendance policies can vary from one class to another. This can create confusion among students and add to varied academic expectations and rigor. Using a systems approach, the leader works to reduce inconsistencies by developing a standardized policy to guide faculty and create consistency across subsystems (e.g., departments). Second, the leader can realign policies, procedures, and communication networks between subsystems to reduce the negative effect of the system in question on other organizational units. This might entail bringing together subsystem representatives to ensure that adjustments are made accordingly. Third, the leader can choose to eliminate connections with the problem subsystem. In extreme circumstances, this disconnect can result in the elimination of a subsystem (e.g., department, program) in order to maintain the integrity of the whole system. Either way, the action made by the other subsystems creates a new and more stable relationship between the subsystems, thereby restoring efficiency and viability to the entire organization.

Systems theory is based on the notion that each subsystem has a unique contribution to the system. Individually, these contributions have little effect, but when the contributions of various subsystems are combined, the result is a more powerful and unified system. In essence, the subsystems could be compared to the individual parts of a machine. By itself, each part has an important role as it relates to the operation of the machine, but it is only in the context of the larger machine that the importance of each part can be completely understood and appreciated (Goldstein, 1986). However, if one part is removed or becomes nonoperational, the machine will not operate properly. With this in mind, a college leader using a systems approach must be informed by several primary factors. First, leaders must understand and familiarize themselves with the specifics of each subsystem, including the subsystem's culture, policies, values, structures, climate, resources, personalities, players, and objectives. Leaders must critically analyze the efficiency of each subsystem by being attuned to subsystem strengths and areas in need of improvement. Second, leaders must possess a firm grasp of the linkages between and relationships among each subsystem, including the resources, policies, procedures, operations, reporting structures, and processes. Leaders must be cognizant of areas where linkages are not in place or where connections are weak. These areas must be identified and addressed in order to improve efficiency between subsystems and, as a result, within the larger system. In all, this will allow leaders to work toward a newly created vision for the system. Finally, leaders must know how each subsystem and the larger system fit within the bureaucratic structure of macrosystems (e.g., local government, state coordinating bodies, state legislatures, federal governments). This requires an understanding of both how the system affects the macrosystems and how the macrosystems impact the system itself.

Under systems theory, organizational success is a by-product of the system and its subsystems (Plowman & Duchon, 2007). Thus, when an individual (e.g., student, faculty member, staff member) or entity (e.g., program, department, division) does not fare well, the responsibility for the outcome is placed on the system. In the community college context, if an institution has low persistence and achievement rates, then the system itself is to blame, not the students served by the system. That said, it should not be assumed that systems theory ignores the role of external factors (e.g., prior academic achievement, income, work-college balance, family responsibilities) or individual competencies in affecting the success of the system. Instead, it suggests that the system itself must be efficient, taking into account both internal and external forces on the system and its affiliates.

There are several primary factors that distinguish systems theory from other theories. First, systems theory is concerned foremost with the system itself. In this light, leaders advocate for the betterment of the system as a whole. This is viewed primarily through the lens of system efficiency and productivity. Second, systems theory is nonlinear and cyclical. Organizations are impacted by continual change from internal and external forces. When this change occurs, leaders must assess the impact of change on the system and, if needed, renegotiate subsystem operations, linkages, and strategic plans. Third, the primary interest of systems theory is to promote the best outcome for the system as a whole. This approach places high priority on system efficiency, not on the subsystems, their subparts, or personnel. The subsystems themselves are merely a means to an end, because the overall goal is the advancement of the organizational mission (McKelvey & Lichtenstein, 2007).

Discussion Questions

Consider the following questions in your analysis of the leadership theory presented in this chapter. In addition, pose your own analytical questions that will aid you in better articulating, analyzing, and critiquing the intricacies of this leadership theory.

- What are the strengths and limitations of systems theory?
- What is the relationship between the leader and the follower in systems theory?
- How is influence gained, maintained, and extended in systems theory?
- How can systems leadership inform the resolution of critical issues faced by community college leaders?
- In what ways have you seen a systems approach employed within your organizational setting?
- How does your preferred leadership style compare to a systems leadership frame?
- In what ways (if any) could your personal leadership be enhanced by systems theory?
- In what way does systems leadership theory compare with and differ from other leadership theories presented in this book?

Regina L. Garza-Mitchell
Associate Vice President for Student Learning
Texas State Technical College

Leading Edge: Connecting Online Education[1]

Background

Leading-Edge Community College (LECC) is a very large suburban community college that services approximately 43,000 students per year, 7,000 of whom take courses online (approximately 40% of online students take their courses only online, with the majority taking them at one or both of the campuses as well as online). The college has been in operation for more than 50 years. Offering more than 200 degree and certificate programs, including five completely online, Leading Edge is one of the largest associate degree–granting institutions in both its state and the nation. LECC also partners with other institutions to offer nearly 50 bachelor's and master's degree options both online and on-ground. The college received approval from its accrediting body to offer all its degree programs online.

LECC is situated within a state that is facing severe economic challenges, including a high unemployment rate. In the service area of the college the unemployment rate is slightly higher than the state average, 7.7% compared with 6.9%, and it is much higher than the national rate of 4.9%. Given the economic climate, the state has offered an incentive to displaced workers allowing them to earn an associate's degree from any community college in the state. The college's surrounding county is one of the largest in the state, with more than 800,000 residents. Despite the high rate of unemployment, the average household income in Leading Edge County is $52,000, compared with a state average of $44,000.

The college has three campuses: Occupational Campus, Career Campus, and Public Safety Campus. Participants in this study represent Occupational and Career campuses. Traditional arts and science courses are offered on the two main campuses along with a host of other degree and certificate programs. Occupational Campus provides most of the technical, engineering, manufacturing, and building-trades programs; Career Campus is centered in a developing area and offers programs in the health and human services fields as well as the culinary arts program; and Public Safety Campus offers public safety programs such as fire and police training. The University Center, in which students can take courses from partner institutions toward earning bachelor's or even master's degrees, is located on Career Campus. In addition to its physical campuses, LECC's online education program has been on an upswing for the past several years.

The college is led by Dr. Anton Darcy, who has invested 29 years of service to the college. Dr. Darcy has spent his entire career at LECC, starting as an adjunct faculty member and making his way up the ranks to president. Dr. Darcy exudes a passion for the college. In talking about being a leading-edge college, he commented, "I think our culture both encourages and, hopefully, recognizes innovation and creativity. I can tell you that as president I don't always want to be the first into something. In fact, we've talked strategically that from time to time we wouldn't mind being the second one in." He is an avid user of technology and because of the widespread usage of the Internet would view it as a disservice if his college did not offer online courses. Dr. Darcy led the successful passage of a technology bond and, later, a voter millage for technology at a time when other community colleges were not successful in passing referendums for funding. These investments allowed the college to move forward without charging a technology fee to students and to provide state-of-the-art equipment for the infrastructures that support online and on-ground technology for the college. Wireless Internet access is available free with no password required, and a computer lab is also available for students and staff on each campus with a proper access card. Most student services are available in completely or partially online format. The college was recognized by a national association as one of the top 10 digital colleges and has received several other awards.

Under Dr. Darcy's leadership, LECC is known for being on the leading—and sometimes the bleeding—edge of technology. The college is known for innovation, particularly in regard to technology, with the term *leading edge* even used in the college mission statement. Although many faculty members and administrators embrace technology, LECC also has its share of employees who prefer to move forward at a slower pace.

The college is supported by more than 1,800 faculty, staff, and administrators, including 200 full-time faculty. College employees are represented by nine unions, with all employees except senior administrators in a bargaining unit. LECC has been unanimously described as a great place to work, and employees take pride in their positions. Both faculty and administrators demonstrate a clear focus on student needs and educational outcomes.

The online education program at LECC started in 1998 with four online, certificated faculty; four courses; and 80 students. Following the first experimental year, the college reached an approved agreement with its faculty union and implemented a three-year pilot program starting in 1999. Early on, a steering committee of faculty, staff, and administrators determined that instructors should complete a college-run training course before being allowed to teach online. This requirement was written into the faculty union contracts. The numbers of courses and instructors grew as instructors completed training and students demonstrated interest. As of the winter 2008 term, a total of 210 online and 11 hybrid course sections were offered. Just over 3,400 students (duplicated) enrolled in completely online courses and 205 students (duplicated) enrolled in hybrid course sections. The online program experienced consistent growth since its inception.

The words *explosive* and *exponential* were most often used to describe the growth of online education at LECC. There has been no decrease in online course enrollment over the past 10 years. If anything, there appears to be a greater demand from students. In the last year alone, enrollment in online courses increased by 22%. A newly installed wait-listing system in 2008 allowed students to add themselves to a wait list if a course was full. Students often opted to be wait-listed for online even when on-ground sections were open.

Since the inception of online offerings, the college instituted rules regarding the number of classes faculty were allowed to teach online (four courses per year), how often students and faculty were required to be online during the week for each course (at least five times per week, with engaging, purposeful, and well-thought contributions), and the amount of time faculty must be on campus (two days per week). Administrators wanted to ensure that there was no significant difference between online and on-ground courses. A campus study showed that learning outcomes were the same, but that online courses had lower persistence rates. The president pushed the expansion of online offerings, but faculty were concerned that they would be unfairly judged by low student performance in classes.

Organizationally, online education is overseen by the learning outreach department, which is responsible for training faculty, staff, and students to use the learning management system (LMS); certification training for online instruction; online student orientation; and a help desk that supports online students, faculty, and staff. The department is situated under the provost and is headed by Vice Provost of Learning Outreach Dr. Nicholas Harvey. The staff in the learning outreach area have seen a fair amount of turnover recently, with a new director, coordinator, and administrative assistant hired within a six-month time period. Coupled with this turnover were changes in the course management system at the college that required faculty to learn new platforms for online classes. This continual change left faculty grumbling.

Other campus offices impacted by the online program are the registrar's office, which handles online as well as on-ground students, student services, financial accounting, and academic affairs. Central to the operations of online education is the technology infrastructure and support. Guidelines required that faculty be certified by the college to teach online by going through a six-week training course. Official contract language and other documents refer to online instructors as facilitators, and "facilitator expectations" for online classes were created. When an online course is developed, the instructor who performs the development must submit a plan identifying course requirements for turning in work including the number of days spent online, communication policy, and a plan for technical problems. Enrollment in online courses is limited to 23 students; this limit is an increase from the initial cap of 18 students and is written into the faculty contract. The LMS is the software program used for online classes. The college is in the process of implementing its fourth LMS in a 10-year period. Changing course management systems is an expensive endeavor that is made possible by the funds from the technology bond and millage. Although faculty appreciate that the changes are made in an effort to continually improve the online experience, even those faculty who consider themselves on the leading edge of technological change admit that it is difficult to learn new software so frequently. They express concern about the learning curve for faculty who are not technologically inclined, and for students who have to negotiate new systems of operation. Yet, faculty are aware of the college's desire to be technologically innovative and those seeking promotion within the college work through these challenges to garner favor with President Darcy.

Statement of the Problem

Online courses have been run as 8-week courses rather than the usual 16. Recently both faculty and administrators have expressed concerns that the condensed format added to the intensity of an online course may be a reason for the high attrition rate in these courses. Some faculty feel that students who are not already well prepared academically face an additional challenge when a course is compressed into half a term. One administrator comments that attrition in online classes causes a financial dilemma as well. The courses are capped at 23 students, fewer than on-ground sections, which might run as many as 100 students per course. Additionally, the drop/add period for online courses is shorter, and students are not allowed to add an online class after the first week. Thus, if students drop a course after it starts, there is a slim chance that the empty seat will be filled by another student. Potential revenue loss, then, is a concern.

Questions

- What are the primary issues in this case? After considering the issues, which group(s) do you think should hold responsibility for addressing the various issues and the urgency of each?
- Create a conceptual model of the flow of operations for the online system considering the interactions among offices, faculty roles, and points of student interaction. How does this differ between online and on-ground course offerings?
- Several changes were written into the faculty contract in regard to online teaching. List these changes and the implications for teaching and learning. What other policy issues must be addressed in regard to online teaching and learning? How might policy be crafted to meet the college's needs but also protect faculty and staff?
- What aspects of curriculum should be considered and addressed before moving forward?
- How is the role of faculty impacted by the shift in regard to technology, teaching, and learning?
- What role should leadership take in defining faculty teaching roles to include technology? What type of faculty development would best support the move to online learning platforms?

Note

1. Case study details were borrowed from research conducted by Regina L. Garza-Mitchell (2008), *Online education in a community college: Individual, group, and organizational perceptions of change* (Unpublished doctoral dissertation). Central Michigan University, Mount Pleasant.

Nevarez & Wood–Systems Leadership Inventory (NW-SyLI)

This leadership inventory is designed to assess the degree to which a leader adheres to a systems leadership frame. Current leaders should reflect on actions that they typically take and perceptions that they hold. For aspiring leaders, conceptualize how your actions in formal (e.g., work) and informal (e.g., home, extracurricular activities) settings may determine your degree of systems leadership influence. Be sure to consider what your actions are, not what you would like them to be. Read the following statements and mark the appropriate response following your instinct; there are no right or wrong answers. Key: 1 = Strongly Disagree, 2 = Disagree, 3 = Somewhat Disagree, 4 = Somewhat Agree, 5 = Agree, and 6 = Strongly Agree.

	Strongly Disagree	Disagree	Somewhat Disagree	Somewhat Agree	Agree	Strongly Agree
1. A primary role of a leader is to facilitate inter-departmental linkages						
2. Inter-organizational communication is vital to organizational success						
3. I am concerned with the success of all departments in my organization						
4. Individual and departmental success is dependent upon the efficiency of the institution						
5. Each organizational unit must work toward a unified goal						
6. Each department/program must have a unique contribution to the greater institution						
7. Organizational success is achieved by each subunit operating at maximum capacity						
8. Leaders should familiarize themselves with the specifics (e.g., role, personnel, policies) of each department in their institution						

9. An inefficient department negatively affects all departments within an institution						
10. Achieving efficiency and productivity within the institution are chief objectives						

Note. This inventory is printed with permission from the Nevarez-Wood Community College Leadership Institute. All rights reserved.

Scoring

To score your responses, add your responses to all of the statements in the inventory. This is your total systems leadership score. Higher scores indicate greater levels of systems orientation, whereas lower scores indicate lower levels of systems orientation. The maximum score possible is 60.

_____ Total Systems Leadership Score

Score Meaning

While the maximum score is 60, many leaders may desire to understand their usage of this framework in comparison with that of other leaders. To facilitate this interest, scores from prior inventory participants were divided into percentile ranges. These percentile ranges allow leaders to understand their score in relation to the scores of other leaders. The percentile ranges are as follows: Low systems orientation (25th percentile or lower), Medium systems orientation (26th to 50th percentile), High systems orientation (51st to 75th percentile), and Very High systems orientation (76th to 99th percentile).

- Low systems orientation: 10–45 points
- Medium systems orientation: 46–49 points
- High systems orientation: 50–53 points
- Very High systems orientation: 54–60 points

Improve Your Systems Leadership Score

System Familiarization. Leaders must understand and familiarize themselves with the specifics of each subsystem that makes the greater system. Recognize the cultures, policies, values, structures, climate, resources, personalities, and goals of the system. Draw a diagram depicting identified outcomes and objectives for each subunit and identify existing linkages.

Collaboration Building. Leaders need to align policies, procedures, and communication networks among subsystems. Bring individuals from various subunits together (e.g., meetings, luncheons, social outings, workshops) to establish and sustain alignments that enforce linkages across subunits.

Assessment of Level of Effectiveness. Leaders need to possess a firm grasp of the linkages among each subunit. Establish a system for monitoring areas where linkages are not in place or where connections are weak. Embed assessment and evaluation into all aspects of the organization and hold respective subunits accountable for meeting identified goals and outcomes (as they align with the organizational mission).

Organizational Success. The primary goal is to promote the best outcome for the system as a whole. The subunits themselves are merely a means to an end. Focus on the impact of change on the system and, if needed, renegotiate subsystem operations to ensure institutional success.

Reliability

Two internal consistency estimates were employed to examine the reliability of the systems leadership inventory: split-half coefficient and coefficient alpha. For the split-half reliability, the scale was divided into equal halves for item equivalency. We took into account the order of the measures; thus, the sequence of items was rotated. One half consisted of items 1, 3, 5, 7, and 9 and the other half consisted of items 2, 4, 6, 8, and 10. The split-half coefficient was .90 and the coefficient alpha was .85. Both procedures illustrated satisfactory reliability. To view this inventory or learn more about using the inventory for research purposes, see http://communitycollegeleadership.net.

Suggested Reading

Nevarez, C., & Wood, J. L. (2011). *Nevarez & Wood–Systems Leadership Inventory (NW-SyLI)*. Sacramento, CA: Nevarez-Wood Community College Leadership Institute.

TRANSFORMATIONAL LEADERSHIP

Transformational leadership denotes a two-phase process. First, followers are guided and encouraged to meet expectations as identified by formal performance agreements (transactional). Second, because of the leader's ability to increase the motivations, morality, and shared meaning of institutional affiliates, achievement beyond expectations is reached (transformational) (Avolio & Bass, 1988; Conger, 1999; Kark & Shamir, 2002). Nevarez and Wood (2010) distinguish this process as "the act of empowering individuals to fulfill their contractual obligations, meet the needs of the organization, and go beyond the 'call of duty' for the betterment of the institution" (p. 59). Transformational leaders are primarily driven by an astute awareness of individual and group psychology. Further, these leaders guide institutional affiliates with a sense of care and support and are truly committed to the self-actualization of institutional affiliates in order to accomplish the institutional mission (serving the community, teaching and learning, student success, lifelong learning). To accomplish this goal, leaders utilize the following array of skills, roles, and behaviors to influence institutional affiliates:

- *Work Ethic.* First and foremost, transformational leaders lead by example through their work ethic, selfless working style, people skills, ability to network, and proficiency in getting the work done (Kark, Shamir, & Chen, 2003; Lowe, Kroeck, & Sivasubramaniam, 1996). This, in turn, establishes a strong sense of legitimacy considering the leader is noted as having "been there" or "done that." The materialized work ethic of the leader and the followers' perceptions of the leader's work ethic afford the leader the ability to gain the commitment and unequivocal support of institutional affiliates. The work commitment displayed, for example, by a community college vice president is made readily available to institutional affiliates. This involves walking the halls, continually engaging in meetings with stakeholders, making efforts to facilitate institutional outcomes, as well as other activities demonstrating that the leader is fully committed to the institution and its mission.

• *Great Communication.* Transformational leaders instill within themselves and the institution a set of grandiose values articulated around an idealistic vision. The leader's ability to garnish the support of institutional affiliates around a unified mission is based on the leader's portrayal of an individual who has a strong sense of self-worth and higher moral judgment. These values affirm and guide institutional affiliates to exceed individual expectations for the greater good of the institution (Avolio, Bass, & Jung, 1999; Pillai & Williams, 2004; Popper & Mayseless, 2003). One example of a transformational leader is a campus president who employs stories and metaphors in his or her speech to illustrate the importance of a particular moment. The purpose of doing so is to motivate institutional affiliates, frequently through emotion, to take action in a certain direction. Often, when this is done, the stories emphasize the importance of heroism, of an institution and its affiliates overcoming great obstacles to actualize its mission. In all, transformational leaders are positive, optimistic, and lead with a sense of hope in accomplishing goals beyond established expectations (Waldman & Bass, 1991; Wang & Rode, 2010).

• *Leading the Way.* Bennis and Nanus (1985) described successful transformational leaders as having the skills to achieve institutional goals through the development of a vision and clear communication of that vision. To be successful, these leaders must secure the trust of institutional affiliates. This trust is needed to guide affiliates in carrying out the institutional vision. Moreover, these leaders develop through professional development activities to ensure that the vision is deployed and enacted within the institution. Buy-in among institutional affiliates is achieved through the leader's genuine efforts to include and sustain the aspirations, thoughts, perceptions, and values of institutional affiliates (Avolio et al., 1999; Bass & Steidlmeier, 1999; Wang & Rode, 2010). This, in turn, ensures the full commitment of institutional affiliates to meet and exceed the institution's needs, goals, and objectives. For instance, a transformational leader is a college dean who uses every opportunity (e.g., college council meetings, commencement addresses, community forums) to engage participants in understanding and aspiring to reach and exceed a set of college/institutional goals. In the case of community colleges, these goals are multifaceted, reflecting the diverse mission of the community college (e.g., open access, student success, comprehensive educational programming, local community needs).

• *Multiskilled Leadership.* One of the cornerstones of the transformational leadership approach focuses on the ability of the leader to transform institutional affiliates so that they can accomplish tasks beyond what is expected of them (Bass, 1998; Bass & Avolio, 1994). In doing so, the leader has a high degree of knowledge and socioemotional intelligence and is well versed in a variety of abilities, styles, and roles. Many of the behaviors and characteristics embodied in charismatic leaders (e.g., being self-confident, displaying moral judgment, having self-worth, being a role model, and having people skills) are tantamount to behaviors displayed by transformational leaders. Charismatic leaders are able to instill in institutional affiliates a sense of trust in the philosophy that they espouse through a heightened sense of association. More simply, leaders' personal identity is unified with their professional identity. These leaders have the ability to use a multitude of skills and behaviors to reach the point where institutional affiliates view work as an expression of their personal being (Barling, Weber, & Kelloway, 1996; Bass & Riggio, 2006). Multiskilled community college leaders are lifelong learners. They regularly seek out professional development opportunities, are immersed in the scholarly literature in their respective areas, and are analytical with respect to reflecting on and critiquing their own experiences. These leaders are committed to examining both "what works" and areas where they or their institutions are in need of further development.

• *Affiliate Development.* The transformational leadership approach seeks to motivate and inspire institutional affiliates to exceed expectations, including the affiliates' expectations for themselves as well as the organization's/leader's expectations for the affiliates (Bass & Riggio, 2006). In doing so, leaders provide a variety of venues, opportunities, and support structures to ensure that affiliates have the proper skills, abilities, disposition, and training to reach their full potential and beyond. In particular, a team-based approach is used to guide efforts. Affiliates' full potential is sought in three primary ways. First, leaders build the conceptual and problem-solving skills of affiliates by encouraging innovation and creativity in solving institutional problems. Second, leaders are attuned to the socioemotional well-being of their affiliates. They continually monitor affiliate behavior and work performance, creating a clear path toward goal accomplishment through a variety of supportive behaviors (e.g., providing advice, allocating resources for professional development, providing one-on-one mentoring). Third, leaders convey high expectations for affiliates. This is primarily accomplished through inspirational motivation. For example, many college leaders consistently encourage institutional affiliates (e.g., faculty, staff) to go beyond their personal self-interest for the betterment of the institution.

Discussion Questions

Consider the following questions in your analysis of the leadership theory presented in this chapter. In addition, pose your own analytical questions that will aid you in better articulating, analyzing, and critiquing the intricacies of this leadership theory.

- What are the strengths and limitations of transformational leadership?
- What is the relationship between the leader and the follower in transformational leadership?
- How is influence gained, maintained, and extended in transformational leadership?
- How can transformational leadership inform the resolution of critical issues faced by community college leaders?
- In what ways have you seen a transformational leadership approach employed within your organizational setting?
- How does your preferred leadership style compare to a transformational leadership frame?
- In what ways (if any) could your personal leadership be enhanced by transformational leadership?
- In what way does transformational leadership theory compare with and differ from other leadership theories presented in this book?

Pamela L. Eddy, Associate Professor
Educational Policy, Planning, and Leadership—Higher Education
Administration
The College of William and Mary

Big Fish in a Small Pond: Leadership Succession at a Rural Community College

Background

Replacing community college leaders remains a central issue for community colleges and their boards as the demographics in the sector point to a massive turnover of leadership over the next decade. Indeed, almost half of current community college presidents are 61 years of age or older. Accompanying the mass exodus of presidents are retirements of chief academic officers (CAOs), which compound leadership succession challenges because many presidents ascend from CAO positions. Likewise, seasoned faculty are retiring in mass, further exacerbating the problem of adequate candidate pools for all levels of leadership positions. Complicating recruitment of new leaders are contextual challenges facing campuses. All colleges are facing fiscal pressures and corresponding demands to increase fund development and entrepreneurial activities. Yet, the differentiated demands on leaders emerge by location, with rural leaders facing problems unique to their locale when compared with their urban counterparts.

Rural community college presidents lead in regions of the country that suffer from low income per capita, aging populations, fewer business and manufacturing opportunities, and lower levels of participation in college attendance among residents. Yet, it is often the college that is looked to for help with economic development and to be a leader in supporting job creation within the region. Moreover, rural community colleges make up the majority (60%) of all community colleges in the nation. It is often difficult to recruit leaders for these colleges because the regions offer little in terms of culture relative to cities and are often geographically isolated. This context is often a tough sell for potential leaders used to more urban living or with partners who are also professionals seeking employment and are challenged by the limited employment options. Fit matters for both the college and the new leader. Rural communities are tight-knit and may distrust "city" people coming in who do not understand local networks or traditions, and who are unfamiliar with rural living.

Petticoat Community College (PCC) is a small rural college with a population of 1,500 students. As with many rural colleges, the bulk of its faculty are full-time, as are the students; the typical full-time student enrolls in 12–15 credit-hours per term. The college opened in 1960 as a branch campus of a nearby four-year university and recently celebrated its 50th anniversary. The current president, Joe Carson, has worked at the college for 43 years, starting as one of the early college faculty and moving up through the ranks. Joe has served as president for 16 years. Steve Elliott, the current vice president of administration likewise has had a long career at the college. Steve has served as VP for the past five years, initially starting his career alongside Joe as a faculty member and also serving a stint as dean of academics. These two leaders serve as the institution's prime source of collective memory and have been instrumental in growing and expanding college operations over time. The two believe strongly in the institution's commitment to access. Joe recently announced his retirement and Steve indicated that he would be retiring the following year to allow for some transition time for the new president. The college has undergone operational changes in addition to the upcoming personnel changes.

Four years ago, the college opened its first set of residence halls. This new campus option allowed for recruitment of students from a wider service area and came at a time when demand for two-year colleges was exceeding capacity. However, the opening of the halls got off to a bumpy start. In the first year, the lack of experience with operations of the residence facilities meant that no restrictions were placed on who could live in the new building. As a result, 35% of the student body in residence were placed on academic probation, with 20% of students withdrawing from the college. An additional 15% of residence students were removed from the hall for disciplinary actions after the first term. New policies emerged requiring a minimum GPA of 2.5 and a zero-tolerance rule for disciplinary infractions. Today, the halls remain full and have witnessed little trouble since the first year. Local students as well as those from across the state see the residence halls as an opportunity to have a "real" college experience. However, students still complain that the shift to a residential campus has not been entirely successful because few events or services are available on the weekends or evenings, and much of the commuter culture and environment remains. Some campus members also are concerned that the opening of the residence halls signals a movement toward more selectivity for admissions and a pressure to offer a community college baccalaureate.

The most recent state assessment of the college highlighted several areas in which the college missed targets. First, graduation rates have been on the decline despite increases in enrollment. The all-time high of 250 graduates occurred a decade ago and each subsequent semester has shown a steady decline. The three-year graduation rate is currently 25%, which still ranks it in the top quarter of rates for all community colleges in the state. Second, student participation in remedial courses has been increasing. Some faculty correlate this increased need for remediation with the opening of the residence halls, asserting that admission standards were lowered in the quest to fill beds in the halls. Finally, internal institutional assessment and data tracking has been lacking. Campus leaders do not know how well PCC students are doing regarding transfer, how remedial education is impacting persistence or graduation rates, or how a newly created academic support course and office has attributed to student success. A survey on student engagement highlighted that there has been less engagement with faculty by commuter students and that not all students have been engaged in collaborative learning outside of class. The lack of faculty mentorship and advising has impacted student transfer experiences as well. The college has been under pressure by the state to increase graduation rates and to increase enrollment.

Statement of the Problem

The announcement of the retirement of Joe Carson provided the board of trustees with an opportunity for change. The concern was determining how to find the "right" leader for the position. Higher education is notorious for its lack of planning for leadership succession compared to the business sector. Nationally, 35% of college presidents obtain their promotions from within the institution. Despite this significant percentage, it remains unknown how much intentional grooming for leadership occurs. Anecdotally, rural colleges tend to promote even greater numbers from within the institution given the college's location and difficulty in attracting national candidates. The emergence of "grow-your-own" leadership development programs in response to difficulties with leadership hiring, however, remains understudied regarding outcomes of the job placement. Leaders who emerge from within the institution are able to hit the ground running, know where all the skeletons are located, and have built-in relationships with major stakeholders.

A year before announcing his retirement, Joe Carson moved Kate Bradley from director of fund development and outreach to the position of provost and dean of the faculty without a national search. She has now served in this position for two years but has retained many of her responsibilities for fund-raising as well. Campus members saw this move as one to position Kate to succeed Joe as president. Kate is a homegrown leader, having started as a student at the college when it first opened in the 1960s, and has worked solely at the college for her entire 30-year career. She understands the issues facing the college and has a strong loyalty base with community and state leaders, key college donors, and the faculty.

The first year of Kate's tenure involved a steep learning curve as a result of her lack of experience in academic leadership. She was well equipped for the administrative functions of creating a schedule, dealing with student advisement, and record keeping, but less prepared for being an academic leader. It had been 15 years since she had completed her doctorate, and she had not kept up with national trends in teaching and learning or recent work on student engagement and developmental education. Her single campus experience rooted her in the traditions of the college and one form of operations. Kate's modus operandi was not to rock the boat. Yet, she has the ability to get things done, especially when it comes to working with faculty to make changes.

As the board of trustees begins its search for a new president, there is much uncertainty on campus. Several current faculty members lobby for Kate to assume the presidency, a position that Joe and Steve also support. She would provide a known commodity for campus members as well as a good bridge from the long-serving tenures of Joe and Steve to the future. The search committee created by the board of trustees consists of members from the local region as well as members in common with the nearby four-year university board of trustees from which it sprang. These fiduciaries wish to bring in a leader who can transition PCC into a leading college ready to address demands of the twenty-first century and to change the perception of the college from a sleepy regional college to a leader in the state. Driving the need for change are state and national pressures to have students obtain degrees or successfully transfer to a four-year university. As at other colleges, PCC is struggling with the best approach to address developmental education. The contextual demands placed on the college require hiring a leader who can manage a delicate balancing act—bringing about change, dealing with a traditional and loyal community base, and addressing resource issues. The board of trustees ultimately wishes to have a change agent on campus to shepherd the process of improving student progress and degree completion. The question at the center of the search is whether this is best accomplished by going with someone who can hit the ground running and who knows the internal landscape or by hiring someone from outside who can bring a fresh perspective.

Tensions surround the search process. On the one hand, campus members are rooted in college traditions and are supportive of Kate Bradley assuming the presidency. On the other hand, the search committee has sent clear messages that change must occur given current demands. The committee would like to hire a change-agent president equipped to navigate the college through the anticipated rocky times facing the state. Evidence of declining graduation rates and increasing student enrollment in developmental courses raises concerns over meeting state and national objectives for college completion. However, bringing in an external leader does not ensure positive outcomes and hiring from the outside may be difficult. Recruiting leaders to rural areas is a challenge given lower pay, fewer cultural amenities, and low levels of campus funding and generally poorer regional economies. PCC is at a crossroads and a critical element influencing future outcomes is the selection of the next president.

Questions

- How should the search committee craft the posting of the opening for president at PCC? In what ways do the leadership competencies outlined by the American Association for Community Colleges influence this job posting?
- What is implied by the board of trustees' desire to bring in a change agent? Is there a particular leadership style that would best support this frame of leading?
- Given the challenges of attracting candidates to positions of rural leadership, how might college administrators plan for leadership succession? How does a rural context influence leadership?

Nevarez & Wood–Transformational Leadership Inventory (NW-TLI)

This leadership inventory is designed to provide a personal profile of leaders' adherence to a transformational leadership frame. Current leaders should reflect on actions that they typically take and perceptions that they hold. Aspiring leaders should consider the actions that they would take if they held a formal leadership position within an organization. Read the following statements and mark the appropriate response; if you find statements difficult to answer, trust your instinct and judgment in selecting the most appropriate for you. Remember that there are no right or wrong answers. Key: 1 = Strongly Disagree, 2 = Disagree, 3 = Somewhat Disagree, 4 = Somewhat Agree, 5 = Agree, and 6 = Strongly Agree.

	Strongly Disagree	Disagree	Somewhat Disagree	Somewhat Agree	Agree	Strongly Agree
1. I am known for being a great communicator						
2. I have established a clear vision and strategic plan						
3. My work ethic motivates others						
4. I am known for "getting the job done"						
5. I have many abilities and talents						
6. I am attuned to the needs of my staff						
7. I model the level of dedication I expect from my staff						
8. I have a high degree of socio-emotional intelligence						
9. My staff regularly exceeds established goals						
10. I encourage the personal development of my employees						
11. I am a lifelong learner						

12. I inspire others with a sense of hope and optimism					
13. I establish high expectations for all my employees					
14. Others are eager to hear what I have to say					
15. My staff works earnestly towards the vision I have established					

Scoring

There are five primary aspects of transformational leaders: work ethic, great communication, leading the way, multiskilled leadership, and affiliate development. To score your responses, add your responses to all of the statements in the inventory. This is your total transformational leadership score. Higher scores indicate greater levels of transformational orientation, whereas lower scores indicate lower levels of transformational orientation. The maximum score possible is 90.

_____ Total Transformational Leadership Score

To better understand how your score relates to the primary components of transformational leadership, (a) add your responses to statements 3, 4, and 7 (this is your total work ethic score); (b) add your responses to statements 1, 12, and 14 (this is your total great communication score); (c) add your responses to statements 2, 9, and 15 (this is your total leading the way score); (d) add your responses to statements 5, 8, and 11 (this is your total multiskilled leadership score); and (e) add your responses to statements 6, 10, and 13 (this is your total affiliate development score). The maximum score for each subscale is 18.

_____ Work Ethic   _____ Great Communication   _____ Leading the Way

_____ Multiskilled Leadership   _____ Affiliate Development

Definitions

Work Ethic. Leading by example through a strong work ethic, selfless working style, people skills, ability to network, and proficiency in getting the work done.

Great Communication. Leading by instilling a set of grandiose values articulated around an idealistic vision.

Leading the Way. Leading with a clear plan and buy-in from institutional affiliates.

Multiskilled Leadership. Leading by exceeding expectations and illustrating a high degree of knowledge and socioemotional intelligence.

Affiliate Development. Leading by providing affiliates with opportunities to develop themselves personally and professionally, which enables them to exceed expectations.

Score Meaning

While the maximum score is 90 total and 18 for each subscale, many leaders may desire to understand their usage of this framework in comparison with that of other leaders. To facilitate this interest, scores from prior inventory participants were divided into percentile ranges. These percentile ranges allow leaders to understand their score in relation to the scores of other leaders. The percentile ranges are as follows: Low transformational orientation (33rd percentile or lower), Medium transformational orientation (34th to 66th percentile), and High transformational orientation (66th to 99th percentile).

- Low transformational orientation: 15–74 points
- Medium transformational orientation: 75–81 points
- High transformational orientation: 82–90 points

Subscales can be interpreted simplistically as low scores and high scores. Based on scores from previous participants, scores of 13 or below are low subscale scores and those 14 or greater represent high usage of the subelements (e.g., work ethic, great communication, affiliate development).

Improve Your Transformational Leadership Score

Work Ethic. Work hard. Transformational leaders lead by example through their work ethic, selfless working style, people skills, ability to network, and get the work done.

Great Communication. Enhance your communication skills. Transformational leaders instill within themselves and the institution a set of values articulated around an idealistic vision. Outline goals that will be necessary to achieve the vision of your institution and communicate this vision often. Use metaphoric language, stories, and analogies to emphasize your arguments. If needed, attend speech development programs to hone your impromptu communication (e.g., Toastmasters).

Leading the Way. Be a role model. Buy-in among institutional affiliates is achieved through the leader's genuine efforts to include and sustain the aspirations, thoughts, perceptions, and values of institutional affiliates. Focus on emulating the behaviors, actions, and dispositions that you wish to see in others.

Multiskilled Leadership. Look for opportunities to learn new skills. Transformational leaders have a high degree of knowledge and socio-emotional intelligence and are well versed in a variety of abilities, styles, and roles. Be a "lifelong" learner by seeking out professional development opportunities offered through your organization, at conferences, and through formal academic course work.

Affiliate Development. Inspire others. Look for ways to learn how to motivate and empower others to exceed their own personal and work expectations. Know what supportive organizational processes are needed to ensure affiliates have the proper skills and knowledge to reach their full potential.

Reliability

The Cronbach's alpha for the total transformational leadership scale is .94. The following coefficient alphas are associated with each subconstruct: .82 (work ethic), .84 (great communication), .85 (leading the way), .78 (multiskilled leadership), and .74 (affiliate development). To view this inventory or learn more about using the inventory for research purposes, see http://communitycollegeleadership.net.

Suggested Reading

Nevarez, C., & Wood, J. L. (2011). *Nevarez & Wood–Transformational Leadership Inventory (NW-TLI)*. Sacramento, CA: Nevarez-Wood Community College Leadership Institute.

12

SYMBOLIC LEADERSHIP

Symbolic leadership uses symbols to motivate followers. Symbols are representations of ideas and indirect allusions to concepts and meanings that the leader wishes to convey. Anything can be a symbol (e.g., buildings, clothing, gestures, metaphors, stories, documents, titles). Symbolic leaders have an advanced understanding of their organization's culture. They propel their efforts by drawing on elements of this culture (symbols) to guide affiliate behaviors and actions (Bolman & Deal, 2003). The symbol itself that is used to communicate an idea is not as important as the meaning that is given to the symbol. Meaning is the interpretation of the message that the symbol portrays, including values, ideas, presumptions, suppositions, principles, and feelings. Symbolic leaders adhere to the notion that meaning is constructed and interpreted from social interactions and messages (Grunig, 1993; Hatch, 2006). As such, all organizational affiliates (e.g., faculty, staff) knowingly or unknowingly influence how messages are understood from the interpretation of symbols. Thus, documents, protocols, policies, procedures, and personal titles are only as important as the meaning attributed by leaders.

Individuals who understand the nuances, complexities, and intricacies of symbols that drive actions and behaviors are most likely to adhere to this leadership approach. For instance, a college public relations officer speaking to the press will be cognizant of the different constituencies receiving the message and will strive to use symbolism to connect to each constituency. The use of symbols can enhance the strength, legitimacy, influence, and positional power of the leader while protecting and projecting the integrity of the college. Symbols also can be used by leaders to control, guide, and facilitate new directions among affiliates and organizational processes.

Symbolic leaders must influence the social reality within the organization. As a result, the goal of symbolic leadership is to properly communicate ideas in a manner in which the follower derives the message that the leader intended to send (Masiki, 2011; McGaughey, 2006). This concept of alignment between the message intended and the message received is the crux of this leadership style. Incorrect alignment can result in confusion or the communication of an alternative meaning not intended, which can diminish the legitimacy of the leader, his or her respective subunit, and the institution as a whole. When messages are properly communicated, they are more easily internalized by followers. Effective leaders using a symbolic style are often seen as inspirational, charismatic, and visionary (Parry & Hansen, 2007), as a result of their use of allegory and metaphor to communicate ideas. These forms of communication are emotive, facilitating a deeper level of imagery.

To ensure that proper message-meaning alignment occurs, leaders must be attuned to a number of factors affecting the interpretation of the message. In particular, this includes organizational culture, social interactions and dynamics, institutional history, and individual dispositions. Symbolic leaders must be insightful, perceptive, and communicative (Bolman & Deal, 2003). Through the effective use of these skills, leaders set a path for personal and organizational success. When leaders are successful in shaping the meaning of an idea, it then becomes the dominant conception. Thus, when alternative meanings are presented, these minor conceptions may have more difficulty gaining traction as they counter the dominant perceptions, imagery, and internalized attitudes and beliefs. In fact, when meanings are fully embraced by organizational affiliates, alternative meanings can be met abruptly and with great opposition. For example, when community college presidents set forth a college slogan, they shape the meaning of what the organizational members are to take away from the slogan. Then, when alternative meanings are presented by faculty, staff, or students, they are less impactful, frowned upon, or easily dismissed, because the dominant meaning has already been constructed. This dominant construction has taken on a life of its own by becoming institutionalized; it guides affiliate practices, thoughts, behaviors, and actions.

There are several primary ways in which symbolic leaders communicate ideas: verbal symbols, physical symbols, structural symbols, relational symbols, ceremonial symbols, and ritual symbols. Verbal symbols refer to the language used by leaders to communicate ideas. In particular, symbolic leaders emphasize the use of metaphors (Hatch, 2006). For example, a college leader could simply tell an employee that he or she is an asset to the organization. While this message is important, it is simplified. This message, however, could be enhanced by a college leader using the words *rock, soldier,* or *pillar* to describe the employee. These words connote enhanced meaning, inspiring strong imagery. Verbal symbols also include the use of allegory (e.g., poems, fables) and stories. Symbolic leaders often use stories from military exploits, Greek mythology, biblical passages, sports, and personal triumph to communicate messages. An example of this would be a leader telling a story of a student graduating after facing incredible odds as a result of a faculty member's mentoring as a means of encouraging other faculty to mentor students.

Symbolic leaders also use physical symbols to convey meaning. Physical symbols are visible representations of an idea, a message, or a value (Masiki, 2011; Tierney, 1989). They can take the form of things such as buildings, posters, clothing, computers, offices, letters, e-mails, and placards. One common example of a physical symbol is the posting of college mission and vision statements throughout the institution's buildings as a means of gathering faculty around these ideas. Another example would be the construction of a massive library building or a learning center to serve as a visible image that the organization is dedicated to student achievement.

Structural symbols are another means that symbolic leaders use to communicate ideas (Tierney, 1989). Structural symbols deal with offices, titles, names, and committees within the institution that are created or revised to convey the importance of an idea. For instance, a college administration that is trying to illustrate its commitment to diversity could establish a presidential committee on diversity, a vice president for diversity, or a chief diversity officer. Or, it could add a person of color to the presidential cabinet. These actions are designed to communicate commitment through the revision of the college structure. Sometimes these positions can be short-lived, because they are developed in a reactive fashion to campus incidents and are designed to demonstrate that the institution is addressing diversity. Further, an administration working to illustrate a commitment to student achievement could establish a presidential taskforce on student achievement. The administration then could invite community leaders, college leaders, faculty, and students to serve on the task force.

Symbolic leaders also use relational symbols. Relational symbols can take the form of verbal or nonverbal interactions designed to convey meaning (Greenfield, 2004; Merriam, 1975). For instance, a program director who wishes to convey a message that he or she is student centered could talk and interact with students during lunch breaks, a time when many faculty, staff, and administrators are on campus and would be likely to observe this interaction. Another example of a relational symbol is leaders who pat subordinates or students on the back when they have done a good job. This action has a dual purpose: illustrating power over individuals while also simultaneously approving their actions.

Many symbolic leaders employ ceremonial symbols to illustrate ideas (Bass, 1993; Cohen, 1976). Ceremonies often take the form of organizational events and activities (e.g., faculty convocations, award nights, new student and faculty luncheons). In general, ceremonies are carefully planned and carried-out events. Sometimes ceremonies are designed to illustrate grandeur through decorations, dress, and the tone of discourse. Other times, ceremonies are purposely simplified in order to illustrate the importance of community and connectedness. For instance, some presidents have monthly "coffee talks" or "tea talks" with students in which the president wears casual apparel and talks in nontechnical terms in an open setting (e.g., coffee shops, campus quad, student union). These ceremonies are designed to illustrate that the president is accessible, open, and student friendly. An example of a more elaborate ceremony is an annual presidential convocation with beautiful decorations, a carefully planned order of events, academic regalia, singing of songs, and a formal lecture. Often, the intended message from such events is one of power, opulence, and control.

Often embedded within ceremonial symbols are ritual symbols. Ritual symbols embody regularly occurring practices (Reitzug & Reeves, 1992). A moment of silence, the singing of the national anthem, the cutting of ribbons, the turning of tassels at graduation, and libations are all examples of rituals. The ritual itself, when it occurs, and how it occurs all convey certain meanings. One example of a ritual is a committee that has a regular moment of silence before it meets to honor a committee member who is deceased. Another example is a newly appointed member of the president's cabinet taking an oath at the beginning of the member's first meeting. This ritual communicates the member's value to the organization; the importance of the member's post; and the commitment of the institution to supporting, enhancing, and facilitating the member's success.

Discussion Questions

Consider the following questions in your analysis of the leadership theory presented in this chapter. In addition, pose your own analytical questions that will aid you in better articulating, analyzing, and critiquing the intricacies of this leadership theory.

- What are the strengths and limitations of symbolic leadership?
- What is the relationship between the leader and the follower in symbolic leadership?
- How is influence gained, maintained, and extended in symbolic leadership?
- How can symbolic leadership inform the resolution of critical issues faced by community college leaders?
- In what ways have you seen a symbolic leadership approach employed within your organizational setting?
- How does your preferred leadership style compare to a symbolic leadership frame?
- In what ways (if any) could your personal leadership be enhanced by symbolic leadership?
- In what way does symbolic leadership theory compare with and differ from other leadership theories presented in this book?

John D. Harrison
NCATE Coordinator and
Assistant Professor of Education
Lincoln Memorial University

Standing at Widler's Gates: Symbolism in Leadership

Background

It was not that long ago that Alex had taken over for Fred, a most beloved figure with more than 30 years of service at South Doyle Community College (SDCC) in Augusta, Georgia. After a long career, Fred had finally retired and was looking forward to spending more time with his grandchildren. As the new director of the English department, Alex was finding that filling the shoes of his predecessor was fraught with unforeseen challenges.

Just a month earlier, Alex walked into Fred's office to be brought up to speed on the departmental operations. Fred had kindly and assuredly expressed his confidence in Alex's abilities and impressed upon him a sense of calm that came from Fred's many years leading the department. Having been with the college only four years, Alex was nervous, yet excited about his appointment as program director. Fred had recommended him, which solidified the opportunity. "Remember what our school's founder said, God rest his soul. 'Today's obstacles do not condemn us to the challenges of our fathers, but lead to glory for future generations,'" Fred had advised. Then he had added, "In other words, don't look at this as the same old challenge and get stuck in a rut. Look at this as an opportunity to strive, achieve, and make the department even better for the students who grace these halls in the future. This will be your time!" Fred was always quick to quote Ivan Westinson, the well-revered and past founder of the college. Whenever there was a difficult situation, or someone in the department or college faced new challenges, Fred knew a quote or story that would set an inspiring tone.

Fred's antics were the stuff of legend at the college. The stories he recounted ranged from those about different colleges to national historical events. In most cases, he would use these stories to gain new resources for the department or to thwart efforts by the college administration to scale back on the department's budget. This was especially apparent four years ago when the department was asked to trim its budget by 15%. Fred went to the dean and gave an impressive speech about the Hershey Chocolate Company and how the owner refused to put in machinery that would have increased production in the plant because it would have cost jobs during the Great Depression. He argued that, like Hershey, there were times when the cut would hurt the two most valuable assets of SDCC: its students and its faculty. With that argument, Fred prevented the department from receiving a massive cut; instead, there was only a 3% cutback. Alex was realizing that the job required much more than knowledge of department operations. Historically, Fred had been able to garner resources through his relationships with members of the board of directors and his charisma.

Although new to SDCC, community college was "old hat" to Alex. He grew up roaming the halls of another community college where his mother served as dean of social sciences. That experience gave him a unique insight into the operations of a college and taught him the nature of politics in an academic setting. Prior to coming to SDCC, he worked as the assistant director of the Learning Center at Walker's State Community College. There he led program development for remedial courses. Alex is a very private person and did not boast about his experience. At 31 years old, he felt that talking about his past work could intimidate the older faculty in the department by branding him as a show-off, cavalier, or simply insecure.

The wealth of Alex's prior experience led to his appointment as the new director at SDCC. Fred was aware of how the experience at the Learning Center uniquely situated Alex to be both student centered and able as a director. However, his appointment was not met with praise from the entire faculty. Unmoved by and/or unaware of his past work history, many of the veteran faculty thought that Alex was too young and inexperienced for the post. They also believed that he was not up to the task of supporting the department like Fred had done for so many years. Questions were circulating: How would he fare if the department's budget was challenged? Would he be able to manage unruly faculty? Could he support faculty who were challenged by students? The most vocal critic was Allen, a professor who had been with the English department for 12 years. On many occasions he openly voiced his displeasure about Alex and had not approved of how he himself had been passed up for the position. Allen felt that he was "naturally" the person who deserved the position given his years at SDCC. The search committee felt differently, noting that although he had the longest service after Fred, he had failed to contribute to the academic community through service. Further, most faculty felt that his social abilities were lacking, at best.

With so much on the line, Alex had to determine how to become established as the leader in the view of the faculty. By reassuring the faculty of his experience, he might be perceived as insecure and seeking faculty approval, and this could certainly undermine the perception of authority that comes with the position of director. Fred's experience taught him that stories, symbols, and traditions could be used to show a person's sense of pride in the institution while also demonstrating intellect and charisma. Now Alex would have to summon his courage, examine the college, and decide how to solidify his position of authority beyond simple titles. Given that faculty and students alike had bought into the images set forth by Fred (seeing themselves as part of an institutional saga), Alex could consider tapping into those stories to further the departmental agenda.

Statement of the Problem

Assume the role of Alex. You have been appointed director of the English department of SDCC, replacing a beloved member of the department, and are facing resistance from some members of the faculty. Symbolism has historically been a central part of conducting business at SDCC. A community college of 9,200 students, SDCC is a centerpiece for the community and is steeped in a long history and rich tradition. The college serves a predominantly White student population (92%), with the remaining students comprising multiple racial/ethnic categories. It is located in the rolling hills of Georgia and is surrounded by a town that has everything from farmland to an internationally renowned PGA golf course. Traditions and historic symbols carry on here through the land, the people, and stories of generations. The following stories, people, traditions, and symbols have been an active part of SDCC and the English department:

- Ivan Westinson, founder of what is now SDCC, was known to carry an embellished cane with him whenever he had an important meeting or when he gave speeches at noted functions. People called his cane the "war baton," because when he had it he was on a mission and out to accomplish it "come what may." Today, leaders in the college tell faculty to grab the "war batons" when an important issue is on the table or when the college has tough decisions to make. It has come to be a point of great pride among the faculty, staff, and students at SDCC.

- Widler's gates are the last remaining landmark of Whittaker College, a small liberal college that was the precursor to SDCC. During the U.S. Civil War, students from the college brought wounded Union soldiers to a makeshift hospital at Widler's house, just beyond the gates. The courage of the students was noted by many historians and became a source of pride for the community. As a result, college presidents have spoken at the gates and capitalized on this imagery.
- The Westinson Achievement Award (WAA) was established in honor of Ivan Westinson. The award is given to those members of the faculty who embody student caring, a commitment to the community (both academic and societal), and stand out as exemplifying the best the college has to offer. This award brings with it a plaque that is represented across the campus, as well as a yearly acknowledgment at the State of the College Presidential Address. Faculty who are awarded the WAA are given special privileges, including leading of the faculty at commencement and access to a special "study" in the campus library, and are given a medallion, which may be worn during the commencement ceremony.
- Litton's soup has become a time-honored symbol of resilience and grass roots at SDCC. John Litton, a groundskeeper and custodian at SDCC, had started a garden in 1911 as a way to mentor local students who were often poor and needed positive guidance. During the Great Depression, many of the students and their families were struggling, often going without meals. John saw the suffering and despair in the community and decided to do something about it. Early one morning he picked vegetables from his garden and made vegetable soup from an old family recipe. He took the soup out to the grounds at the front of the campus. Walking through the street of the campus he rang a bell, announcing that the meal was prepared. Litton hosted a weekly soup meal for the local community throughout the entirety of the depression. Students, their families, and members of the community gathered on the front lawn and were served Litton's soup. Today, John Litton's garden is still maintained by the groundskeeping staff and by students from the local high school's 4-H club. Each year, a staff member who exemplifies community service is chosen to walk through campus with students as he or she rings the same bell that John Litton rang, announcing that a meal has been prepared. They

then serve Litton's soup on the front grounds. The event has become not only a part of SDCC tradition, but also a celebrated part of the history in the state.

- Within the English Department, Fred had started a tradition of inviting faculty to meet on Wednesday for brunch at the student center. Fred believed that faculty should be seen in student areas so that students would be aware that their professors were interested in being around them and seeing the things that they were doing. He also felt that having the brunch gave the department's faculty an opportunity to discuss their scholarly activities, class issues, and accomplishments and build camaraderie. These brunches became a staple in the department with Fred always leading the initial discussions.

As you enter your position consider symbolism and its importance at SDCC when addressing the following questions:

- What issues are you facing as you assume the director position at SDCC?
- How has your appointment been challenged and in what ways might the displeasure of faculty manifest itself? Consider both active and passive means of aggression.
- How might you use symbolism and the symbols outlined in the case study in order to solidify your position in the department? Consider the different types of symbolism from the chapter when forming your response.
- Are there ways that Fred may be able to assist you in this transition? If so, what do you perceive as the benefits and drawbacks of his assistance?
- When addressing the resistance to your appointment in the department, what form of a speech or planned discussion should you consider? Assume that the speech or discussion will be held during your first departmental brunch. Be creative. Use symbolism and SDCC's history as a reference point.
- When developing your speech or planned discussion, what are important political and practical issues that must be considered? How can symbolism play a part in addressing these issues? Are there unwritten rules that guide this discussion?

Nevarez & Wood–Symbolic Leadership Descriptor Inventory (NW-SLDI)

This leadership inventory is designed to assess the degree to which a leader adheres to a symbolic frame. Current leaders should reflect on actions that they typically take and perceptions that they hold. For aspiring leaders, conceptualize how your actions in formal (e.g., work) and informal (e.g., home, extracurricular activities) settings may determine your degree of leadership influence. Be sure to consider what your actions are, not what you would like them to be. Read the following statements and mark the appropriate response following your instinct; there are no right or wrong answers. Key: 1 = Strongly Disagree, 2 = Disagree, 3 = Somewhat Disagree, 4 = Somewhat Agree, 5 = Agree, and 6 = Strongly Agree.

	Strongly Disagree	Disagree	Somewhat Disagree	Somewhat Agree	Agree	Strongly Agree
1. I have an advanced understanding of my organization's culture						
2. I have established important traditions for my department/ organization						
3. I often use stories to propel my arguments						
4. Others perceive me as charismatic						
5. I embrace and use our organization's culture to drive our efforts						
6. I often communicate ideas through the use of metaphors						
7. I am cognizant of my organization's values						
8. Others believe that I am visionary						
9. I reinforce important values and principles by making them visible (i.e., posting an organizational mission statement, displaying core values)						

10. Others perceive me as inspirational							
11. Leaders must embrace organizational tradition							
12. I often use metaphors (e.g., pillar, soldier, rock, lion) to describe valued employees							
13. I guide my staffs' behavior by drawing upon elements of our organization's culture							
14. My leadership draws upon the culture of my organization							

Note. This inventory is printed with permission from the Nevarez-Wood Community College Leadership Institute. All rights reserved.

Scoring

To score your responses, add your responses to all of the statements in the inventory. This is your total symbolic leadership score. Higher scores indicate greater levels of symbolic orientation, whereas lower scores indicate lower levels of symbolic orientation. The maximum score possible is 84.

_____ Total Symbolic Leadership Score

Score Meaning

While the maximum score is 84, many leaders may desire to understand their usage of this framework in comparison with that of other leaders. To facilitate this interest, scores from prior inventory participants were divided into percentile ranges. These percentile ranges allow leaders to understand their score in relation to the scores of other leaders. The percentile ranges are as follows: Low symbolic orientation (25th percentile or lower), Medium symbolic orientation (26th to 50th percentile), High symbolic orientation (51st to 75th percentile), and Very High symbolic orientation (76th to 99th percentile).

- Low symbolic orientation: 14–58 points
- Medium symbolic orientation: 59–64 points

- High symbolic orientation: 65–68 points
- Very High symbolic orientation: 69–84 points

Improve Your Symbolic Leadership Score

Communication. Learn how to use policies, procedures, and personal titles as a symbolic communication tool to drive actions and behaviors among followers. Be purposeful in expressing insights, perceptions, and experiences.

Emotional Intelligence. Develop the skills to be insightful and develop meaning and interpretations of a variety of symbols for followers through demonstrating insightfulness, finesse, and intelligence.

Symbolic Rituals. Develop your knowledge of rituals and ability to use them as a communication tool to connect with people. Use these rituals to communicate ideas and values and to secure support.

Powerful Symbols. Learn how to communicate ideas in a manner in which the follower deeply connects with the message you intended to send. In doing so, symbolic leaders are seen as inspirational, charismatic, and visionary. Use metaphoric and symbolic language when communicating ideas.

Reliability

Two internal consistency estimates were employed to examine the reliability of the symbolic leadership inventory: split-half coefficient and coefficient alpha. For the split-half reliability, the scale was divided into equal halves for item equivalency. We took into account the order of the measures; thus, the sequence of items was rotated. One half consisted of items 1, 3, 5, 7, 9, 11, and 13 and the other half consisted of items 2, 4, 6, 8, 10, 12, and 14. The split-half coefficient was .88 and the coefficient alpha was .91. Both procedures illustrated satisfactory reliability. To view this inventory or learn more about using the inventory for research purposes, see http://communitycollegeleadership.net.

Suggested Reading

Nevarez, C., & Wood, J. L. (2011). *Nevarez & Wood–Symbolic Leadership Inventory (NW-SLI).* Sacramento, CA: Nevarez-Wood Community College Leadership Institute.

13

TRANSFORMATIVE LEADERSHIP

Transformative leadership is a social justice–oriented approach undergirded by notions of democracy (e.g., opportunity, equity, fairness, freedom). Leaders using this framework seek to identify, challenge, and redress issues of marginalization, power, privilege, and subjugation in society (Keddie, 2006; Weiner, 2003). In particular, transformative leaders are concerned with inequities facing diverse student communities, recognizing that these inequities are part of a larger societal context that reinforces hierarchical structures of dominance and power. For these leaders, racism, sexism, ableism, classism, and other forms of marginality are viewed as evils that *must* be deconstructed and countered. Given this perspective, transformative leaders are concerned with outcomes (Dantley, 2003; Mertens, 2007). They desire to construct new sociocultural realities that are liberating and emancipatory in nature. For instance, transformative leaders do not adhere to the notion that the achievement gap is a by-product of underserved students, their families, or their communities (Brown, 2004; McLaughlin, 1989). Rather, they reject this approach as a deficit model, pointing to inequities in school funding and resources needed to acquire curricular materials; laws that serve to benefit and reify the powerful over the powerless; personnel who are not reflective of the communities in which they serve; as well as historical and contemporary oppression among governing bodies, state policy makers, and those in the dominant majority (Glanz, 2007; Shields, 2003).

Transformative leaders embrace diversity, seeing differences (e.g., socioeconomic, cultural, linguistic) as an asset, which better position institutions to meet the needs of their constituencies. Leaders who embrace this particular theory are progressive in that they acknowledge the world is evolving, and that organizations must deconstruct traditional ideologies, practices, and values (Quantz, Rogers, & Dantley, 1991). Instead, they enact new models, realities, policies, and structures that can address the inequalities plaguing society. This process of deconstructing old realities and constructing new ones is guided by notions of equity, social justice, democracy, liberation, and emancipation (Shields, 2010). Key to the practice of transformative leadership is the process of engaging communities, building inclusive structures, and encouraging collaboration from all stakeholders, particularly those who have experienced marginalization (Bennis, 1986; Capper, 1989; Davis, 2006).

Transformative leaders are, at their core, advocates for others. However, astute transformative leaders understand that maintaining control of their emotions and understanding what battles are "worth" fighting is important because they must maintain and advance their credibility, positional authority, and psychological well-being. Further, they must gain buy-in from others who may not possess the same values. While working toward the creation of a "just" college, too many transformative leaders lose sight of functioning with a balanced approach that allows them to focus on long-term structural change as opposed to short-term superficial change. Transformative leaders must understand that they are challenging the dominant power (status quo) and that in doing so missteps can result in negative outcomes (e.g., termination, marginalization, burnout, loss of respect). However, some transformative leaders are able to successfully cultivate the transformation of their institutions. In achieving these goals, their efforts are furthered by several core leadership orientations. As articulated by Kose (2009), successful transformative leaders are visionary leaders, learning leaders, structural leaders, cultural leaders, and political leaders.

As *visionaries*, transformative leaders work collectively with college personnel to establish a unified vision. The core element of this vision is the pursuit of educational equity. As such, leaders institutionalize the values of equity into every aspect of the institution, including hiring practices, the curriculum, strategic planning, allocation of resources, college initiatives, programming, and community engagement. Transformative leaders anticipate, plan, and develop a multiplicity of institutional practices and efforts that are purposively designed to "transform" the institution. This transformation is intended to make the institution more responsive to issues of equity and social justice. Visionary leaders recognize that advancing equity-oriented practices is a long-term commitment, which will benefit marginalized groups and society as a whole (e.g., economically, socially, politically). These leaders strive to address the needs of a changing demographic population that is becoming increasingly diverse in multiple areas (e.g., level of academic preparation, language acquisition, variation in student socioeconomic status). This vision is facilitated by data-driven decision-making processes, which inform all organizational components (e.g., mission, objectives, functions) needed to actualize the unified vision. For community college leaders, the vision guiding their practice provides broader postsecondary educational opportunities for all individuals in society (Nevarez & Wood, 2010). Transformative community college leaders seek out this vision in two primary ways: (a) they advocate for greater proportional representation among students, faculty, staff, and administration in each respective unit of the organization; and (b) they demand that equity of outcomes for each respective group be reached. For instance, many community college leaders are concerned with the dismal success of minority male students. An example of a transformative leader is one who, in seeking broader postsecondary education for all, establishes strategic initiatives, programs, and policies that are meant to increase the success of minority male students in multiple areas (e.g., enrollment, remediation, persistence, graduation, transfer).

Transformative leaders are also *learning leaders*. They are in tune with the realities of their constituencies given their continual dialogue and engagement with the people (e.g., staff, students, community members) whom they serve. These leaders are concerned with gaining critical input from all groups, particularly those who are typically excluded from such conversations, in order to advocate for better outcomes for these individuals. As learners, these leaders understand the importance of negotiating multiple contexts. Thus, as individuals who are committed to rectifying inequities, transformative leaders immerse themselves into the practice of their formal positions as well as the underserved communities for which they advocate. These leaders do so because they recognize that understanding the needs of the underserved is best approached through interactions, conversations, and allegiance to those communities. Further, transformative leaders understand the importance of experiential knowledge. They are critical in their reflection of actions, behaviors, mandates, policies, structures, and all other mechanisms that do, or could potentially, create inequities. Critical reflection allows leaders to advocate for parity in future activities as well as to engage in reparative justice, whereby past wrongs are made "right."

Given that transformative leaders are *structurally* oriented, they are concerned with meeting the formal obligations of their respective posts (e.g., developing materials, scheduling, budgeting). Transformative leaders must be respected bureaucrats, possessing the credibility and knowledge needed to guide their colleges toward parity. These leaders are concerned with organizational efficiency and effectiveness, recognizing that organizational health is imperative for positioning colleges to address educational inequities. For instance, organizations with defunct policies, processes, and procedures are unable to levy their human and financial resources to address marginalization. An example of a structural leader is a community college dean who ensures that proper protocols and responsibilities are established within all divisions. When organizational structures are clear, leaders are able to identify misaligned processes or communication channels, which may further sustain inequities.

Cultural leadership is an important consideration for transformative leaders. As culturally proficient individuals, these leaders are aware of and respect multiple cultural worldviews. In doing so, these leaders are cognizant of their own beliefs, values, and attitudes. They are continually introspective, challenging themselves and others to recognize and counter inequities. Further, transformative leaders are aware of oppressive sociocultural norms and microaggressions (subtle discriminatory practices), which serve to reinforce the marginalization of nondominant groups. Using this awareness, they imbue principles and values of social justice to seek equity and embrace organizational diversity. As such, diversity is viewed as a virtue, a strength used to reach organizational goals. Therefore, transformative leaders affirm principles of diversity throughout the college, its subunits, and the local communities in which they serve.

Given the *political* nature of organizations, transformative leaders have an enhanced understanding of institutional politics. They are aware of the power players, stakeholders, resources, relationships, and other factors that shape institutional policy, processes, and structures. This awareness is used to build agreements and relationships that better enable the leader to counter hegemonic organizational structures, people, and culture. A core component of this leadership approach is the ability to consider actions, multiple steps in advance. This encompasses the skill to predict the behaviors, actions, and motivations of others. An example of a transformative leader who possesses political aptitude is a retention program director at a community college who anticipates how budget constraints will motivate key players at the decision-making table to cut program funding. By foreseeing potential cuts, this leader (a) moves toward securing funding from outside resources (e.g., foundations, special-interest groups, private donors) that will sustain the academic and social support for students most in need; and (b) negotiates future transactions with supportive parties to obtain their support in minimizing or eliminating potential cuts.

Discussion Questions

Consider the following questions in your analysis of the leadership theory presented in this chapter. In addition, pose your own analytical questions that will aid you in better articulating, analyzing, and critiquing the intricacies of this leadership theory.

- What are the strengths and limitations of transformative leadership?
- What is the relationship between the leader and the follower in transformative leadership?
- How is influence gained, maintained, and extended in transformative leadership?
- How can transformative leadership inform the resolution of critical issues faced by community college leaders?
- In what ways have you seen a transformative leadership approach employed within your organizational setting?
- How does your preferred leadership style compare to a transformative leadership frame?
- In what ways (if any) could your personal leadership be enhanced by transformative leadership?
- In what way does transformative leadership theory compare with and differ from other leadership theories presented in this book?

Leila González Sullivan
Former President, Essex Community College–Baltimore County
Adjunct Professor
North Carolina State University

The Blogging College

Background

Seven Hills Community College (SHCC) is located in an older city in the Northeast that has received waves of European immigrants since the early 1900s. Its original manufacturing base attracted many new arrivals who could find jobs that allowed them to raise families and live reasonably comfortably. Gradually the earlier immigrant populations have moved out to the surrounding suburbs, and their children have become prosperous members of the middle class.

Today the city has a large population of African American residents as well as a growing Hispanic community comprising primarily Central Americans. Unfortunately, many of the original manufacturing jobs have moved elsewhere or overseas, and the current residents are struggling economically. The competition between African Americans and Hispanics for jobs has created tensions in the local area, particularly because there is a sense that undocumented people are taking some of the jobs. There is also resentment about the need for English as a second language in the schools and about the Hispanic residents' heavy use of social services.

Established in 1959, SHCC has its primary campus in an aging building complex at the crossroads of the city's two main streets. There is also a newer satellite campus located in one of the northwestern suburbs. The student body at the downtown location is largely African American and Hispanic, whereas the satellite campus serves a predominantly White student body. This year, student enrollment reached an all-time high, with 12,675 full- and part-time credit students. There were also 9,444 noncredit students enrolled for vocational courses or enrichment. As in community colleges across the country, roughly two thirds of the students are female and one third male. Student demographic breakouts show 52% African American, 25% Hispanic, 11% White, 4% Asian, and 8% Other or Unknown. The faculty, most of whom are tenured, are 70% White and 60% female, with an average age of 48 years.

SHCC offers a standard array of AA, AS, and AAS degrees, as well as numerous certificates. Its most popular degree programs are pre-nursing and criminal justice. Recently, it received a large grant to develop Homeland Security and engineering technician degrees, and it is exploring a gaming option under the computer technician degree. The college enjoys considerable support from the local community because it is the only higher education institution in the city itself and many residents see it as the only educational option.

Statement of the Problem

You are the provost and chief academic officer (CAO) of SHCC and the first Latina woman in the history of the college to serve in this role. You are aware that growing numbers of people in the college community enjoy communicating about campus matters via various social media. Generally, you check the blog site each day when you have a few minutes just to see what issues and topics are being posted. This morning you discover that one of the bloggers has posted a message informing all readers that Jorge Maldonado, a new student at SHCC, is a convicted felon and should not be allowed to enroll in the institution. The message is signed "Concerned." Because there is much curiosity on campus about the blog, it is likely that many administrators, faculty, and students will see this post very soon, if they have not already done so.

A bit troubled, you scroll on through the posts and find one marked "URGENT." This message is signed by one of the faculty members in the psychology department, who states that many people are convicted felons and that they should not be prohibited from enrolling in college. This could be read as an admission that Jorge Maldonado is, in fact, a convicted felon and that the administration knew this when he enrolled.

Next are two messages, one from another faculty member and one from a student, expressing concern about the safety of their persons and property if a criminal is allowed on campus. After all, they note, because the college is in an urban setting and is relatively open to the public, there have been problems before. These messages are followed by a "flamer" from the president of the LatinLink Student Organization, who sees the initial message as "just one more example of the rampant racism on campus." He intends to demand that the administration investigate this incident and several other "racist" incidents that he describes.

You then turn to your phone messages and find just what you expect: calls from the LatinLink president and from Jorge Maldonado's lawyer. Both want to meet with you as soon as possible. You know it is only a matter of time before a well-connected reporter for the local newspaper (they all keep an eye on the social media) will call to find out about the latest tempest at SHCC.

The situation has some personal and professional implications for you as a Latina woman who is relatively new to the position of provost. You are aware that the local Hispanic community expects you, as one of their own, to be an advocate for their concerns and interests even though you try to be balanced in your approach. And, because you are Latina, the African American leaders in the city have been watching suspiciously to see if you will favor the Hispanics. The college president is aware of this tension and has been hoping that your appointment will help maintain the peace. The ability to manage problems such as the one resulting from the blog postings could affect your overall effectiveness and will undoubtedly be considered in your performance evaluation.

The following background information may be of help as you address the situation:

- *Social Media.* The college has just begun to explore these new communication tools. A few of the departments and student organizations have created Facebook pages and now there is the college blogging site, which permits any member of the college community to post, provided the message is not lewd or defamatory. For the moment, a member of the public relations department has been assigned to monitor the blog site and notify the director of public relations if anything questionable is posted. The director can decide whether the material should be removed. A committee has been established to develop an official policy for social media, but its work is just beginning. Among other aspects of such a policy, the committee has had some heated discussions about free speech versus college image. In addition, the public relations department has established guidelines for the college brand in print materials, but it is not clear whether these could or should be extended to social media.

- *Student Privacy Issues.* When Jorge Maldonado enrolled, although he did disclose his previous status on the application form as requested, he certainly did not expect his status as a former felon to be publicized, given the Family Educational Rights and Privacy Act (FERPA). It may not be possible to determine who posted the original message—whether an administrator, a faculty member, or a student. However, the post by the psychology professor gives rise to additional questions about student privacy and free speech. Did this person simply offer his own personal views on the matter or was he speaking for the college? Does the college have a policy on who speaks for the institution? In either case, how might the community view the professor's post?

- *Community Relations.* Both the internal and external communities of the college could be affected by this blogging incident. In addition, as is often the case with an event of this sort, other concerns have attached themselves to the initial trigger. Among the internal community, the issues of personal safety and racism have surfaced and may have long-term effects if not addressed. In the surrounding external community, questions about safety and racism may now arise as well, especially in light of the fact that there is some resentment over the growing Hispanic presence because it may be negatively affecting local schools and job opportunities. Community concerns arising from this incident could affect student recruitment, fund-raising, and general goodwill for the college in its service area.

As provost and CAO, you realize that this situation must be addressed rapidly in order to avoid serious and possibly long-term consequences. Consider the following questions in choosing your course of action:

- Who needs to be informed of the situation and/or involved in addressing the various intertwined issues?
- Are there additional factors that you need to consider in resolving this case, and what information might you still need to gather?
- Does FERPA apply in this case, and how can the exposed student be protected, if necessary?
- What should be done about the use of social media by campus community members?
- What, if anything, should be done about the psychology professor's comment?

- How will you address the racism accusation raised by the student leader of LatinLink?
- What are the public relations implications of the case?
- On a personal and professional level, what should you do about the expectations of you as provost among the Hispanic and African American community leaders?

Nevarez & Wood–Transformative Leadership Inventory (NW-TrLI)

This leadership inventory is designed to assess the degree to which a leader adheres to a transformative frame. Current leaders should reflect on actions that they typically take and perceptions that they hold. For aspiring leaders, conceptualize how your actions in formal (e.g., work) and informal (e.g., home, extracurricular activities) settings may determine your degree of transformative leadership influence. Be sure to consider what your actions are, not what you would like them to be. Read the following statements and mark the appropriate response following your instinct; there are no right or wrong answers. Key: 1 = Strongly Disagree, 2 = Disagree, 3 = Somewhat Disagree, 4 = Somewhat Agree, 5 = Agree, and 6 = Strongly Agree.

	Strongly Disagree	Disagree	Somewhat Disagree	Somewhat Agree	Agree	Strongly Agree
1. I am committed to social justice						
2. I challenge the "status quo"						
3. I advocate against marginalization						
4. I am concerned with inequities facing diverse student communities						
5. Traditional ideologies, practices and values must be deconstructed						
6. I am dedicated to advancing educational equity						
7. I view culture as a benefit not a disadvantage						
8. I have a strong will when it comes to overcoming injustice						

Note. This inventory is printed with permission from the Nevarez-Wood Community College Leadership Institute. All rights reserved.

Scoring

To score your responses, add your responses to all of the statements in the inventory. This is your total transformative leadership score. Higher scores indicate greater levels of transformative orientation, whereas lower scores indicate lower levels of transformative orientation. The maximum score possible is 48.

_____ Total Transformative Leadership Score

Score Meaning

While the maximum score is 48, many leaders may desire to understand their usage of this framework in comparison with that of other leaders. To facilitate this interest, scores from prior inventory participants were divided into percentile ranges. These percentile ranges allow leaders to understand their score in relation to the scores of other leaders. The percentile ranges are as follows: Low transformative orientation (25th percentile or lower), Medium transformative orientation (26th to 75th percentile), and High transformative orientation (76th percentile to 99th percentile).

- Low transformative orientation: 8–38 points
- Medium transformative orientation: 39–44 points
- High transformative orientation: 45–48 points

Improve Your Transformative Leadership Score

Community Engagement. Transformative leaders enact new models, realities, policies, and structures that address the inequalities plaguing institutions. Regularly and often raise issues of equity and social justice as topics of discussion in various forums and meetings. Provide opportunities for the underserved to have a voice in decision making, and be attentive to identified concerns.

Vision. Review policies and regulations of the institution to facilitate educational equity. Transformational leaders institutionalize the values of equity into every aspect of the institution, including hiring practices, the curriculum, strategic planning, and community engagement. Develop a written document (in concert with others) that outlines the institution's vision for addressing inequities.

Cultural Proficiency. Ask yourself, "How well do I appreciate the values, traditions, and competencies of diverse individuals?" Transformative leaders are aware of and respect multiple cultural worldviews. They are continually introspective, challenging themselves and others to counter inequities. Engage yourself in reading books, articles, and reports on cultural relevancy, racial/gender microaggressions, and globalization.

Political Awareness. Be aware of opportunities that you might use to your advantage to facilitate an equity agenda. Transformative leaders are aware of the power players, stakeholders, resources, relationships, and other factors that shape institutional policy. Become more attuned to when to play your cards and when to hold them.

Reliability

Two internal consistency estimates were employed to examine the reliability of the transformative leadership inventory: split-half coefficient and coefficient alpha. For the split-half reliability, the scale was divided into equal halves for item equivalency. We took into account the order of the measures; thus, the sequence of items was rotated. One half consisted of items 1, 3, 5, and 7 and the other half consisted of items 2, 4, 6, and 8. The split-half coefficient was .93 and the coefficient alpha was .90. Both procedures illustrated satisfactory reliability. To view this inventory or learn more about using the inventory for research purposes, see http://communitycollege leadership.net.

Suggested Reading

Nevarez, C., & Wood, J. L. (2011). *Nevarez & Wood–Transformative Leadership Inventory (NW-TrLI).* Sacramento, CA: Nevarez-Wood Community College Leadership Institute.

REFERENCES

American Association of Community Colleges. (2005). *Competencies for community college leaders.* Washington, DC: Author.

Apple, M. (2000). *Official knowledge: Democratic education in a conservative age.* New York, NY: Routledge.

Astley, W. G., & Van de Ven. (1983). Central perspectives and debates in organizational theory. *Administration Science Quarterly, 28*(2), 245–273.

Avolio, B. J., & Bass, B. M. (1988). Transformational leadership, charisma, and beyond. In J. G. Hunt, B. R. Baliga, H. P. Dachler, & C. A. Schriesheim (Eds.), *Emerging leadership vistas* (pp. 29–49). Lexington, MA: Lexington Books.

Avolio, B. J., Bass, B. M., & Jung, D. I. (1999). Re-examining the components of transformational and transactional leadership using the Multifactor Leadership Questionnaire. *Journal of Occupational and Organizational Psychology, 72,* 441–462.

Avolio, B. J., & Locke, E. A. (2002). Contrasting different philosophies of leader motivation: Altruism versus egoism. *Leadership Quarterly, 13,* 169–191.

Barling, J., Weber, T., & Kelloway, E. K. (1996). Effects of transformational leadership training on attitudinal and financial outcomes: A field experiment. *Journal of Applied Psychology, 81,* 827–832.

Barney, J. B. (1986). Organizational culture: Can it be a source of sustained competitive advantage? *Academy of Management Review, 11*(3), 656–665.

Bass, B. M. (1985). *Leadership and performance beyond expectation.* New York, NY: Free Press.

Bass, B. M. (1990). *Bass & Stogdill's handbook of leadership: Theory, research, and managerial applications* (3rd ed.). New York, NY: Free Press.

Bass, B. M. (1993). Transformational leadership and organizational culture. *Public Administration Quarterly, 17*(1), 112–121.

Bass, B. M. (1998). *Transformational leadership: Industry, military, and educational impact.* Mahwah, NJ: Lawrence Erlbaum.

Bass, B. M., & Avolio, B. J. (1994). *Improving organizational effectiveness through transformational leadership.* Thousand Oaks, CA: SAGE.

Bass, B. M., & Riggio, R. E. (2006). *Transformational leadership.* Mahwah, NJ: Lawrence Erlbaum.

Bass, B. M., & Steidlmeier, P. (1999). Ethics, character, and authentic transformational leadership behavior. *Leadership Quarterly, 10,* 181–217.

Bauer, T. N., & Green, S. G. (1996). The development of leader-member exchange: A longitudinal test. *Academy of Management Journal, 39,* 1538–1567.

Beane, J. A., & Apple, M. W. (1999). *Democratic schools. Lessons from the chalk face.* Buckingham, UK: Open University Press.

Beckner, W. (2004). *Ethics for educational leaders.* Boston, MA: Pearson.

Bell, D. (1950). Notes on authoritarian and democratic leadership. In A. W. Gouldner (Ed.), *Studies in leadership* (pp. 395–408). New York, NY: Harper & Row.

Bennis, W. (1986). Transformative power and leadership. In T. J. Sergiovanni & J. E. Corbally (Eds.), *Leadership and organizational culture: New perspectives on administrative theory and practice* (pp. 64–71). Chicago, IL: University of Illinois Press.

Bennis, W. G., & Nanus, B. (1985). *Leaders: The strategy for taking charge.* New York: Harper & Row.

Bensman, J., & Rosenberg, B. (1960). The meaning of work in bureaucratic society. In M. R. Stein, A. J. Vidich, & D. M. White (Eds.), *Identity and anxiety: Survival of the person in mass society* (pp. 181–197). Glencoe, IL: Free Press.

Blanchard, K. H., Zigarmi, D., & Nelson, R. B. (1993). Situational leadership after 25 years: A retrospective. *Journal of Leadership Studies, 1,* 22–36.

Blank, W., Weitzel, R., & Green, S. G. (1990). A test of situational leadership theory. *Personnel Psychology, 43,* 579–597.

Bolman, L. G., & Deal, T. E. (2003). *Reframing organizations: Artistry, choice, and leadership.* San Francisco, CA: Jossey-Bass.

Brown, K. M. (2004). Leadership for social justice and equity: Weaving a transformative framework and pedagogy. *Educational Administration Quarterly, 40*(1), 77–108.

Bush, E. C. (2004). *Dying on the vine: A look at African American student achievement in California community colleges* (Doctoral dissertation). Available from ProQuest Dissertations and Theses database. (UMI No. 3115606)

Bush, E. C., & Bush, L. (2010). Calling out the elephant: An examination of African American male achievement in community colleges. *Journal of African American Males in Education, 1*(1), 40–62.

Cairns, T. D., Hollenback, J., Preziosi, R. C., & Snow, W. A. (1998). Technical note: A study of Hersey and Blanchard's Situational Leadership Theory. *Leadership and Organizational Development Journal, 19,* 113–116.

Caldwell, C., Shapiro, J. P., & Gross, S. J. (2007). Ethical leadership in higher education administration: Equality vs. equity. *Journal of College Admission, 195,* 14–19.

Capper, C. A. (1989). *Transformative leadership: Embracing student diversity in democratic schooling.* Madison, WI: University of Wisconsin.

Carver, J., & Carver, M. (1994). *A new vision for board leadership: Governing the community college.* Washington, DC: Association of Community College Trustees.

Chance, P. L., & Chance, E. W. (2002). *Introduction to educational leadership and organizational behavior: Theory into practice.* Larchmont, NY: Eye on Education.

Cohen, A. (1976). *Two-dimensional man: An essay on the anthropology of power and symbolism in complex society.* Berkeley, CA: University of California Press.

Conger, J. A. (1999). Charismatic and transformational leadership in organizations: An insider's perspective on these developing streams of research. *Leadership Quarterly, 10,* 145–170.

Court, M. (2003). Towards democratic leadership: Co-principal initiatives. *International Journal of Leadership in Education, 6*(2), 161–183.

Dahl, R. A. (1989). *Democracy and its critics.* New Haven, CT: Yale University Press.

Dantley, M. (2003). Critical spirituality: Enhancing transformative leadership through critical theory and African American prophetic spirituality. *International Journal of Leadership in Education, 6*(1), 3–17.

Davis, S. H. (2006). Influencing transformative learning for leaders. *School Administrator, 63*(8), 1.

Delgado, R. (Ed.). (1995). *Critical race theory: The cutting edge.* Philadelphia, PA: Temple University Press.

Deluga, R. J. (1998). Leader-member exchange quality and effectiveness ratings: The role of subordinate-supervisor conscientiousness similarity. *Group and Organization Management, 23,* 189–216.

Dienesch, R. M., & Liden, R. C. (1986). Leader-member exchange model of leadership: A critique and further development. *Academy of Management Review, 11,* 618–634.

DiPadova, L. (1996). Towards a Weberian management theory: Lessons from Lowell Bennion's neglected masterwork. *Journal of Management History, 2*(1), 59–74.

DiPadova, L., & Brower, R. (1992). A piece of lost history: Max Weber and Lowell L. Bennion. *American Sociologist, 23,* 37–73.

Dooley, K. (1997). A complex adaptive systems model of organization change. *Nonlinear Dynamics, Psychology, and the Life Sciences, 1,* 69–97.

Eddy, P. L. (2010). *Leadership: A multidimensional model for leading change.* Sterling, VA: Stylus.

Erdogan, B., Kraimer, M. L., & Liden, R. C. (2004). Work value congruence and intrinsic career success: The compensatory roles of leader-member exchange and perceived organizational support. *Personnel Psychology, 57,* 305–332.

Erdogan, B., Liden, R. C., & Kraimer, M. L. (2006). Justice and leader-member exchange (LMX): The moderating role of organizational culture. *Academy of Management Journal, 49,* 395–406.

Evans, M. G. (1970). The effects of supervisory behavior on the path-goal relationship. *Organizational Behavior and Human Performance, 5*, 277–298.

Evans, M. G. (1996). R.J. House's path-goal theory of leader effectiveness. *Leadership Quarterly, 7*, 305–309.

Fernandez, C. F., & Vecchio, R. P. (1997). Situational leadership theory revisited: A test of an across-jobs perspective. *Leadership Quarterly, 8*, 67–84.

Fishkin, J. (1991). *Democracy and deliberation: New directions for Democratic reform.* New Haven, CT: Yale University.

French, J., & Raven, B. H. (1959). The bases of social power. In D. Cartwright (Ed.), *Studies of social power* (pp. 150–167). Ann Arbor, MI: Institute for Social Research.

Fulk, J., & Wendler, E. R. (1982). Dimensionality of leader-subordinate interactions: A path-goal investigation. *Organizational Behavior and Human Performance, 30*, 241–264.

Gaus, G. (2001). What is deontology? Part one: orthodox views. *Journal of Value Inquiry, 35*, 27–42.

Gerstner, C. R., & Day, D. V. (1997). Meta-analytic review of leader-member exchange theory: Correlates and construct issues. *Journal of Applied Psychology, 82*, 827–844.

Gilligan, C. (1982). *In a different voice: Psychological theory and women's development.* Cambridge, MA: Harvard University Press.

Girodo, M. (1998). Machiavellian, bureaucratic, and transformational leadership styles in police managers: Preliminary findings of interpersonal ethics. *Perceptual and Motor Skills, 86*(2), 419–428.

Glanz, J. (2007). On vulnerability and transformative leadership: An imperative for leaders of supervision. *International Journal of Leadership in Education, 10*(2), 115–135.

Goldstein, J. (1986). A far-from-equilibrium systems approach to resistance to change. *Organizational Dynamics, 15*(1), 5–20.

Goodson, J. R., McGee, G. W., & Cashman, J. F. (1989). Situational leadership theory: A test of leader prescriptions. *Group and Organizational Studies, 14*, 446–461.

Graeff, C. L. (1983). The situational leadership theory: A critical review. *Academy of Management Review, 8*, 285–291.

Graeff, C. L. (1997). Evolution of situational leadership theory—A critical review. *Leadership Quarterly, 8*, 153–170.

Graen, G. B., Alvares, K. M., Orris, J. B., & Martella, J. A. (1970). Contingency model of leadership effectiveness: Antecedent and evidential results. *Psychological Bulletin, 74*, 285–296.

Graen, G. B., & Uhl-Bien, M. (1995). Relationship-based approach to leadership: Development of leader-member exchange (LMX) theory of leadership over 25 years: Applying a multi-level multi-domain perspective. *Leadership Quarterly, 25,* 219–247.

Green, R. L. (2005). *Practicing the art of leadership: A problem-based approach to implementing the ISSLC standards* (2nd ed.). Upper Saddle River, NJ: Merrill Prentice Hall.

Green, R. L. (2010). *The four dimensions of principal leadership: A framework for leading 21st century schools.* Boston, MA: Allyn & Bacon.

Greenfield, W. D. (2004). Moral leadership in schools. *Journal of Educational Administration, 42*(2), 174–196.

Greve, H. R. (2007). Power and glory: Concentrated power in top management teams. *Organization Studies, 28*(8), 1197–1221.

Grunig, L. A. (1993). Image and symbolic leadership: Using focus group research to bridge the gaps. *Journal of Public Relations Research, 5*(2), 95–125.

Haiman, F. S. (1951). *Group leadership and democratic action.* Boston, MA: Houghton-Mifflin.

Hall, R. H. (1963). The concept of bureaucracy: An empirical assessment. *American Journal of Sociology, 69*(1), 32–40.

Harrison, J. A. (1998). School governance: Is the clash between teachers and principals inevitable? *Journal of Educational Administration, 36*(1), 59–82.

Hatch, M. J. (2006). *Organization theory: Modern, symbolic, and postmodern perspectives.* Oxford, UK: Oxford University Press.

Haus, M., & Sweeting, D. (2006). Local democracy and political leadership: Drawing a map. *Political Studies, 54,* 267–288.

Hellriegel, D., & Slocum, J. W. (2009). *Organizational behavior* (12th ed.). Mason, OH: Southwest Cengage Learning.

Hirsch, P. M., & Lounsbury, M. (1997). Putting the organization back into organizational theory: Action, change, and the "new" institutionalism. *Journal of Management Inquiry, 6*(1), 79–88.

Houghton, J. D., & Yoho, S. K. (2005). Toward a contingency model of leadership and psychological empowerment: When should self-leadership be encouraged? *Journal of Leadership and Organizational Studies, 11*(4), 65–83.

House, R. J. (1971). A path-goal theory of leader effectiveness. *Administrative Science Quarterly, 16,* 321–338.

House, R. J. (1996). Path-goal theory of leadership: Lessons, legacy, and a reformulated theory. *Leadership Quarterly, 7*(3), 323–352.

House, R. J., & Mitchell, T. R. (1974). Path-goal theory of leadership. *Journal of Contemporary Business, 3,* 81–97.

Hoy, W. K., & Miskel, C. G. (2005). *Educational leadership and reform.* Greenwich, CT: Informational Age.

Jackall, R. (1988). *Moral mazes: The world of corporate managers.* New York, NY: Oxford University Press.

Jermier, J. M. (1996). The path-goal theory of leadership: A subtextual analysis. *Leadership Quarterly, 7*(3), 311–317.

Jones, G. R. (2007). *Organizational theory, design, and change* (5th ed.). New York, NY: Pearson.

Kark, R., & Shamir, B. (2002). The dual effect of transformational leadership: Priming relational and collective selves and further effects on followers. In B. J. Avolio & F. J. Yammarino (Eds.), *Transformational and charismatic leadership: The road ahead* (pp. 67–91). Amsterdam, Netherlands: JAI.

Kark, R., Shamir, B., & Chen, G. (2003). The two faces of transformational leadership: Empowerment and dependency. *Journal of Applied Psychology, 88,* 246–255.

Keddie, A. (2006). Gender and schooling: Frameworks for transformative social justice. *Discourse: Studies in the Cultural Politics of Education, 27*(3), 399–415.

King, B. G., Felin, T., & Whetten, D. A. (2010). Finding the organization in organizational theory: A meta-theory of the organization as a social actor. *Organization Science, 21*(1), 290–305.

Kose, B. W. (2009). The principal's role in professional development for social justice: An empirically-based transformative framework. *Urban Education, 44*(6), 628–663.

Kotter, J. (1985). *Power and influence: Beyond formal authority.* New York, NY: Free Press.

Kouzes, J. M., & Posner, B. Z. (2003). *Leadership challenge* (3rd ed.). San Francisco, CA: Jossey-Bass.

Kroll, M. J., & Pringle, C. D. (1985). Individual differences and path-goal theory. The role of leader effectiveness. *Southwest Journal of Business and Economics, 2*(3), 11–20.

Kutner, B. (1950). Elements and problems of democratic leadership. In A. W. Gouldner (Ed.), *Studies in leadership* (pp. 459–467). New York, NY: Harper & Row.

Lewin, K. (1950). The consequences of an authoritarian and democratic leadership. In A. W. Gouldner (Ed.), *Studies in leadership* (pp. 409–417). New York, NY: Harper & Row.

Liden, R. C., & Maslyn, J. M. (1998). Multidimensionality of leader-member exchange: An empirical assessment through scale development. *Journal of Management, 24,* 43–72.

Liden, R. C., Sparrowe, R. T., & Wayne, S. J. (1997). Leader–Member Exchange theory: The past and potential for the future. *Research in Personnel and Human Resources Management, 15,* 47–119.

Lowe, K. B., Kroeck, K. G., & Sivasubramaniam, N. (1996). Effectiveness correlates of transformational and transactional leadership: A meta-analytic review of the MLQ literature. *Leadership Quarterly, 7,* 385–425.

Marion, R. (1999a). *The edge of the organization: Chaos and complexity theories of formal social systems.* Thousand Oaks, CA: SAGE.

Marion, R. (1999b). Organizational extinction and complex systems. *Emergence, 1*(4), 71–96.

Marion, R., & Uhl-Bien, M. (2001). Leadership in complex organizations. *Leadership Quarterly, 12*(4), 389–418.

Masiki, T. (2011). Academic visual identity (AVI): An act of symbolic leadership. *Journal of Marketing for Higher Education, 21*(1), 85–105.

Maxcy, S. J. (2002). *Ethical school leadership.* Lanham, MD: Scarecrow Press.

McDade, S. A. (1988). *Leadership in higher education.* ERIC Digest. Washington, DC: ERIC Clearinghouse on Higher Education.

McGaughey, J. L. (2006). Symbolic leadership: Redefining relations with the host organization. *New Directions for Adult and Continuing Education, 56,* 39–50.

McGregor, D. (1960). *The human side of enterprise.* London, UK: McGraw-Hill.

McKelvey, B., & Lichtenstein, B. (2007). Leadership in the four stages of emergence. In J. Hazy, J. Goldstein, & B. Lichtenstein (Eds.), *Complex systems leadership theory* (pp. 93–108). Boston, MA: ISCE.

McLaughlin, D. (1989). Power and the politics of knowledge: Transformative leadership and curriculum development for minority language learners. *Peabody Journal of Education, 66*(3), 41–60.

McLeod, C. (2003). Toward a restorative organization: Transforming police bureaucracies. *Police Practice and Research, 4*(3), 361–377.

Mechanic, D. (1964). Source of power of lower participants in complex organizations. *Administrative Science Quarterly, 7*(3), 349–364.

Merriam, A. H. (1975). Symbolic action in India: Gandhi's nonverbal persuasion. *Quarterly Journal of Speech, 61*(3), 290–306.

Mertens, D. M. (2007). Transformative considerations: Inclusion and social justice. *American Journal of Evaluation, 28*(26), 86–90.

Mintzberg, H. (1979). *The structuring of organizations.* Englewood Cliffs, NJ: Prentice Hall.

Nevarez, C., & Wood, J. L. (2010). *Community college leadership and administration: Theory, practice, and change.* New York, NY: Peter Lang.

Nevarez, C., & Wood, J. L. (2012). A case study framework for community college leaders. *Community College Journal of Research and Practice, 36*(4), 310–316.

Noddings, N. (2003). *Caring: A feminine approach to ethics and moral education* (2nd ed.). Berkeley, CA: University of California Press.

Norris, W. R., & Vecchio, R. P. (1992). Situational leadership theory: A replication. *Group and Organizational Management, 17*, 331–342.

Northouse, P. G. (2007). *Leadership: Theory and practice.* Thousand Oaks, CA: SAGE.

Nye, J. S. (2008). *The power to lead.* New York, NY: Oxford University Press.

Parry, K. W., & Hansen, H. (2007). The organizational story as leadership. *Leadership, 3*(3), 281–300.

Pateman, C. (1970). *Participation and democratic theory.* Cambridge, UK: Cambridge University Press.

Pateman, C. (1983). Feminism and democracy. In G. Duncan (Ed.), *Democratic theory and practice* (pp. 204–217). Cambridge, UK: Cambridge University Press.

Pellegrini, E. K., & Scandura, T. A. (2006). Leader-member exchange (LMX), paternalism and delegation in the Turkish business culture: An empirical investigation. *Journal of International Business Studies, 37*, 264–279.

Pellegrini, E. K., Scandura, T., & Jayaraman, V. (2010). Cross-cultural generalizability of paternalistic leadership: An expansion of leader-member exchange theory. *Group & Organization Management, 35*(4), 391–420.

Pillai, R., & Williams, E. A. (2004). Transformational leadership, self-efficacy, group cohesiveness, commitment, and performance. *Journal of Organizational Change Management, 17*, 144–159.

Plowman, D. A., & Duchon, D. (2007). Emergent leadership: Getting beyond heroes and scapegoats. In J. Hazy, J. Goldstein, & B. Lichtenstein (Eds.), *Complex systems leadership theory* (pp. 109–128). Boston, MA: ISCE.

Popper, M., & Mayseless, O. (2003). Back to basics: Applying a parenting perspective to transformational leadership. *Leadership Quarterly, 14*, 41–65.

Pratt, M. W., Skoe, E. E. A., & Arnold, M. L. (2004). Care reasoning development and family socialisation patterns in later adolescence: A longitudinal analysis. *International Journal of Behavioral Development, 28*(2), 139–147.

Quantz, R. A., Rogers, J., & Dantley, M. (1991). Rethinking transformative leadership: Toward democratic reform of schools. *Journal of Education, 173*(3), 96–118.

Reitzug, U. C., & Reeves, J. E. (1992). Miss Lincoln doesn't teach here: A descriptive narrative and conceptual analysis of a principal's symbolic leadership behavior. *Educational Administration Quarterly, 28*(2), 185–219.

Schriesheim, C. A., & DeNisi, A. S. (1981). Task dimensions as moderators of the effects of instrumental leadership: A two-sample replicated test of path-goal leadership theory. *Journal of Applied Psychology, 66*, 589–597.

Schriesheim, C. A., & Neider, L. L. (1996). Path-goal leadership theory: The long and winding road. *Leadership Quarterly, 7*, 317–321.

Schriesheim, C. A., & Von Glinow, M. A. (1977). The path-goal theory of leadership: A theoretical and empirical analysis. *Academy of Management Journal, 20*, 398–405.

Schriesheim, J. F., & Schriesheim, C. A. (1980). A test of the path-goal theory of leadership and some suggested directions for future research. *Personnel Psychology, 33*, 349–370.

Shapiro, J. P., & Gross, S. J. (2008). *Ethical educational leadership in turbulent times: (Re)solving moral dilemmas.* New York, NY: Lawrence Erlbaum.

Shapiro, J. P., & Stefkovich, J. A. (2005). *Ethical leadership and decision making in education: Applying theoretical perspectives to complex dilemmas* (2nd ed.). Mahwah, NJ: Lawrence Erlbaum.

Shields, C. M. (2003). *Good intentions are not enough: Transformative leadership for communities of difference.* Lanham, MD: Scarecrow/Technomics.

Shields, C. M. (2010). Transformative leadership: Working for equity in diverse contexts. *Educational Administration Quarterly, 46*(4), 558–589.

Skoe, E. E. A. (2010). The relationship between empathy-related constructs and care-based moral development in young adulthood. *Journal of Moral Development, 39*(2), 191–211.

Skoe, E. E. A., Cumberland, A., Eisenberg, N., Hansen, K., & Perry, J. (2002). The influences of sex and gender-role identity on moral cognition and prosocial personality traits. *Sex Roles, 46*(9–10), 295–309.

Skoe, E. E., & Marcia, J. E. (1991). A care-based measure of morality and its relation to ego identity. *Merrill-Palmer Quarterly, 37*, 289–304.

Smith, T. (2006). *Ayn Rand's normative ethics.* Cambridge, UK: Cambridge University Press.

Starratt, R. (2003). Democratic leadership theory in late modernity: An oxymoron or ironic possibility? *Ethical Dimensions in School Leadership, 1*(1), 13–31.

Stoker, G. (1991). *The politics of local government* (2nd ed). Basingstoke, UK: Macmillan.

Stoker, G. (1995). Regime theory and urban politics. In D. Judge (Ed.), *Theories of urban politics* (pp. 54–71). London, UK: SAGE.

Strike, K. A., Haller, E. J., & Soltis, J. F. (2005). *The ethics of school administration* (3rd ed.). New York, NY: Teachers College Press.

Swenson, R. (1991). Order, evolution, and natural law: Fundamental relations in complex system theory. In C. Negoita (Ed.), *Cybernetics and applied systems* (pp. 125–147). New York, NY: Marcel Dekker.

Tierney, W. (1989). Symbolism and presidential perceptions of leadership. *The Review of Higher Education, 12*(2), 153–166.

van Staveren, I. (2007). Beyond utilitarianism and deontology: Ethics in economics. *Review of Political Economy, 19*, 21–35.

Vecchio, R. P. (1987). Situational leadership theory: An examination of a prescriptive theory. *Journal of Applied Psychology, 72*, 444–451.

Vecchio, R. P., Bullis, R. G., & Brazil, D. M. (2006). The utility of situational leadership theory: A replication in a military setting. *Small Group Research, 37,* 407–424.

Waldman, D. A., & Bass, B. M. (1991). Transformational leadership at different phases of the innovation process. *Journal of High Technology Management Research, 2,* 169–180.

Wang, P., & Rode, J. C. (2010). Transformational leadership and follower creativity: The moderating effects of identification with leader and organizational climate. *Human Relations, 63,* 1105–1128.

Weber, M. (1947). *The theory of social and economic organizations* (T. Parsons, Trans.). New York, NY: Free Press.

Weiner, E. J. (2003). Secretary Paulo Freire and the democratization of power: Toward a theory of transformative leadership. *Educational Philosophy and Theory, 35*(1), 89–106.

Wofford, J. C., & Liska, L. Z. (1993). Path-goal theories of leadership: A meta-analysis. *Journal of Management, 19,* 857–876.

Woods, P. A. (2004). Democratic leadership: Drawing distinctions with distributed leadership. *International Journal of Leadership in Education, 7*(1), 3–26.

Yukl, G. (1989). *Leadership in organizations* (2nd ed.). Englewood Cliffs, NJ: Prentice Hall.

Yun, S., Cox, J., & Sims, H. P. (2006). The forgotten follower: A contingency model of leadership and follower self-leadership. *Journal of Managerial Psychology: Self-leadership, 21*(4), 374–388.

ABOUT THE AUTHORS

Carlos Nevarez, PhD, is director and professor of the Doctorate in Educational Leadership Program at California State University, Sacramento. Dr. Nevarez is also the executive editor of *Journal of Transformative Leadership and Policy Studies*. His research lies at the intersection of leadership, organizational change, and educational equity, and his work on Latinos in education has received national recognition. He served as one of the founders and chairs of the American Educational Research Association Special Interest Group: Multicultural/Multiethnic Education: Research, Theory, and Practice and continues to serve on the leadership team as chair emeritus, providing direction, guidance, and insight to the SIG. His book *Community College Leadership and Administration: Theory, Practice, and Change* (Peter Lang Publishing, 2010), which he coauthored with J. Luke Wood, has quickly become one of the leading textbooks on preparing community college leaders and administrators.

J. Luke Wood, PhD, is assistant professor of administration, rehabilitation, and postsecondary education at San Diego State University (SDSU). Dr. Wood is codirector of the Minority Male Community College Collaborative (M2C3), a national project of the Interwork Institute at SDSU. He is also coeditor of *Journal of African American Males in Education* and chair of the Multicultural & Multiethnic Education special-interest group of the American Educational Research Association. His work has focused on the development of academic programs designed to cultivate ethical leaders focused on issues of social justice and educational equity. This has included service as the doctoral program director at Lincoln Memorial University and the co-coordinator of the Arizona Education Policy Fellowship. His research on Black males examines factors (e.g., social, psychological, academic, environmental, institutional) that impact their outcomes (e.g., persistence, achievement, attainment, transfer, labor market outcomes) in community colleges.

Rose Penrose is the interim vice principal at Laguna Creek High School in the Elk Grove Unified School District. She previously served there as the academic program coordinator. Penrose's work enables her to apply leadership theory to practice as she coaches, manages, and supervises programs and staff at the secondary level. She earned an MA in educational leadership from California State University, Sacramento, and a BA in English from the University of California, Davis. She also holds a California Administrative Credential and Teaching Credential. Penrose has more than 20 years of education experience. She spent several years working with education policy and politics at the state level before entering the teaching profession in 2003 and subsequently becoming an administrator.

Also Available from Stylus

Community College Leadership
A Multidimensional Model for Leading Change
Pamela L. Eddy
Foreword by George R. Boggs

"Pamela L. Eddy's [book] deserves our time for two simple reasons: first, the multidimensional model for leading change transcends community colleges and is applicable broadly within and beyond education; and, second, the author's thoughtful inclusion of vignettes and case studies provides the day-today grounding to make her model relevant to readers of all professions. Yes, community college readers have the advantage of knowing many of the leadership challenges firsthand and will be more interested than most in sections such as 'Challenges of Community College Leadership,' but this book adds sufficiently to leadership literature that it should find itself on the bookshelves of professionals across education and the private sector."—***The Department Chair***

"Pamela Eddy has done seminal work in creating a multidimensional model for leading change in the community college. This is an excellent resource for all aspiring community college leaders as well as those serving as senior leaders in our institutions. The book is well written and contains an exceptional combination of theory to practice ideas and thoughts. It is sure to become required reading in community college leadership development programs."—***Larry H. Ebbers***, *Community College Leadership Programs, Iowa State University*

Fundraising Strategies for Community Colleges
The Definitive Guide for Advancement
Steve Klingaman

"Steve Klingaman's results-oriented strategies will benefit anyone ready to take a fresh look at their community college's fundraising. He provides a systematic approach to assessing what's effective, tackles barriers and myths, and offers countless practical, doable strategies that will instill confidence and produce positive results."—***Paul Heaton***, *Director of the Center for Community College Advancement, The Council for Advancement and Support of Education (CASE)*

Fundraising Strategies for Community Colleges is the only comprehensive development guide to focus on community college fund raising. Written for development professionals, college presidents, board members, trustees, faculty leaders, and other college leadership, this book is an essential, practical guide that fills a critical gap in the market.

Topics include:

- Strategies used at one two-year college that raised $50 million over ten years
- 75 boxed tips on the details that matter most
- How to create an institutional commitment to advancement
- How to enhance the advancement function
- How to build an effective foundation board that gives
- How to grow the Annual Fund with sustainable, repeatable gifts
- Secrets top universities use to close major gifts
- Continuous quality improvement techniques to improve results year after year.

Gateway to Opportunity?
A History of the Community College in the United States
J. M. Beach
Foreword by W. Norton Grubb

"Beach's focus on the community college as an evolving social institution offers a perspective not found in earlier literature . . . For readers interested in the history of the community college as a social institution, this book offers a concise treatment of its subject with numerous references to many important articles and texts that have reported on change and practice at the community college. Approaching the community college as a social institution offers a perspective that should be used more often to better understand the development, changes, and dilemmas in the history of this uniquely American experiment in post-secondary education."—***Community College Review***

"The question of whether or not [community colleges] expand access by democratizing higher education or constrain access by diverting students away from higher-prestige institutions is one that is continually and hotly debated . . . J.M. Beach critically and comprehensively reexamines this well-worn territory in an effort to connect the origins of community colleges with the institutions that they have become in today's higher education milieu . . . Beach elucidates provocative questions that educators, colleges, and policy makers must consider."—***Harvard Educational Review***

22883 Quicksilver Drive
Sterling, VA 20166-2102

Subscribe to our e-mail alerts: www.Styluspub.com